George Augustus Cobbold

Religion in Japan - Shintoism, Buddhism, Christianity

George Augustus Cobbold

Religion in Japan - Shintoism, Buddhism, Christianity

ISBN/EAN: 9783743311602

Manufactured in Europe, USA, Canada, Australia, Japa

Cover: Foto ©Lupo / pixelio.de

Manufactured and distributed by brebook publishing software (www.brebook.com)

George Augustus Cobbold

Religion in Japan - Shintoism, Buddhism, Christianity

SAMMON OF CHION-IN, KYOTO.

Frontispiece.] [See page 61.

RELIGION IN JAPAN:

SHINTOISM—BUDDHISM—CHRISTIANITY.

BY

GEORGE A. COBBOLD, B.A.,

PEMBROKE COLLEGE, OXFORD.

WITH ILLUSTRATIONS.

PRINTED UNDER THE DIRECTION OF THE TRACT COMMITTEE.

LONDON:
SOCIETY FOR PROMOTING CHRISTIAN KNOWLEDGE.
NORTHUMBERLAND AVENUE, W.C.; 43, QUEEN VICTORIA STREET, E.C.
BRIGHTON: 135, NORTH STREET.
NEW YORK: E. & J. B. YOUNG & CO.
1894.

CONTENTS.

	PAGE
INTRODUCTORY	11
I. SHINTOISM	18
II. BUDDHISM	30
III. BUDDHISM IN JAPAN	47
IV. BUDDHISM AND CHRISTIANITY	67
V. CHRISTIANITY IN JAPAN	90

LIST OF ILLUSTRATIONS.

I. SAMMON OF CHION-IN, KYOTO   *Frontispiece*

II. GROUP OF SHINTO PRIESTS WITH TORII   *To face page*   24

III. DAIBUTSU AT KAMAKURA   ,,   ,,   39

IV. KIYOMIZU-DERA, KYOTO   ,,   ,,   61

V. STATUES OF KWANNON, SAN-JU-SAN-GEN-DO   ,,   64

VI. ALTAR OF SAN-JU-SAN-GEN-DO   ,,   ,,   66

VII. GUARDIAN NIO   ,,   ,,   68

VIII. PAGODA AT NIKKO   ,,   ,,   71

IX. PLAN OF TEMPLE AT IKEGAMI   ,,   ,,   72

X. A BUDDHIST PRIEST   ,,   ,,   75

XI. SKETCH MAP OF JAPAN   ,,   ,,   98

RELIGION IN JAPAN.

INTRODUCTORY.

It may well be questioned whether, in the course of a like period of time, any country has ever undergone greater transitions, or made more rapid strides along the path of civilization than has Japan during the last quarter of a century. A group of numerous islands, situated on the high-road and thoroughfare of maritime traffic across the Pacific, between the Eastern and Western hemispheres, and in area considerably exceeding Great Britain and Ireland,—Japan, until thirty years ago, was a *terra incognita* to the rest of the world; exceeding even China in its conservatism and exclusiveness. And now, within a space of some five-and-twenty years, such changes have come about as to have given birth to the expression,—"the transformation of Japan." The more conspicuous of these changes are summed up by a recent writer in the following words: —"New and enlightened criminal codes have been enacted; the methods of judicial procedure have been entirely changed; thoroughly efficient systems of police, of posts, of telegraphs, and of national education have been organized; an army and a navy modelled after Western patterns have been formed; the finances of the Empire have been placed on a sound basis; railways, roads, and harbours have been constructed; an efficient mercantile marine has sprung into existence; the jail system has been radically improved; an extensive scheme of local government has been put into operation; a competitive civil service has been organized; the whole fiscal system has been revised; an influential and widely-read newspaper press has grown up with extraordinary rapidity; and government by parliament has been substituted for monarchical absolutism[1]." At the present day, an Englishman travelling in Japan is constantly meeting numbers of his countrymen, intent on either business or pleasure; while at all the principal cities and places of resort, handsome new hotels, fitted in Western style, are to be found. The Mikado may be seen driving through his Capital in a carriage that would not be out of place in the Parks of London or Paris; and at Court ceremonies European dress is *de rigueur*. English is taught in all the better-class schools, and at the Universities the works of such authors as Bacon, Locke, Macaulay, Darwin, John Stuart Mill, Herbert Spencer, are in constant request with the students. In short, on every side evidence is

[1] Sir Edwin Arnold's *Seas and Lands*, chap. xxvii.

afforded, that be it for better or for worse, the old order is fast changing and giving place to new.

The circumstances which have brought about these wonderful changes can only be very briefly indicated here. It was towards the middle of the sixteenth century that Japan first came into contact with the Western world; the first traders to arrive being the Portuguese, who were followed some sixty years later by the Dutch, and in 1613 by a few English ships. To all of these alike a hospitable reception appears to have been accorded; nor is there any doubt that Japanese exclusiveness was a thing of subsequent growth, and that it was based only on a sincere conviction that the nation's well-being and happiness would be best consulted by refusing to have dealings with the outer world. And indeed, that the Japanese should have arrived at this decision is by no means to be wondered at; their first experience of foreign intercourse having been singularly unfortunate. The unhappy breach, which eventually led to Japan entirely closing her ports to foreign traffic, was, it would seem, due partly to the attitude of harsh intolerance and general interference adopted by certain of the Roman Catholic missionaries, who by this time had arrived in the country: and partly to the insinuations made by the Dutch that the Portuguese were aiming at territorial aggrandizement. Anyhow, in 1624, Japan was entirely closed to foreign trade, save for some concessions,—accompanied by the severest restrictions,—permitted to the Dutch; no foreigners were allowed to enter, and no natives to leave, the empire; the missionaries were expelled, and Christianity was prohibited under pain of death. The Japanese, as has been said, "suspected everybody and shut out the world." Previous to this crisis the English had retired; but when, in 1673, our country sought to resume friendly relations, the connexion existing between the English and Portuguese courts proved an insuperable obstacle [1]. Subsequent overtures made in 1849, were courteously but firmly rejected; though the period of Japan's isolation was, as later events proved, almost at an end. In 1853, the Government of the United States despatched a fleet across the Pacific, under the command of Commodore Perry, to insist upon the surrender of a policy which, it was urged, no one nation of the world had a right to adopt towards the rest. Whether the arguments with which this position was advanced would of themselves have prevailed, is impossible to say; but since it was evident that should words fail, sterner measures would be resorted to, Japan had no choice but to submit. Treaties were accordingly concluded, first with the United States, and subsequently with England

[1] Charles II's queen, it will be remembered, was Katharine of Braganza.

and other European powers; by virtue of which a few ports were grudgingly opened, and Japanese subjects permitted to engage in commercial transactions with the outside world. For the first few years, it is certain that a strong feeling of suspicion and dislike towards foreigners was rife; but in 1868 events occurred which brought about a complete change in the whole situation. For some six hundred years a dual system of government had existed in Japan. On the one hand, was the Mikado, supposed to trace a lineage of unbroken descent from the gods, and accorded a veneration semi-divine, but living in seclusion at the city of Kyoto, with such powers of administration as he still retained confined to matters of religion and education. On the other hand, was the Shogun, or Tycoon, the acknowledged head of a feudalism, which, while nominally recognizing the Mikado's authority, had usurped the sovereign power, and really governed the country. But in 1868, the altered circumstances in which Japan found herself brought about a revolution. The ancient nobility were filled with indignation and disgust at the Tycoon so far violating Japanese tradition as to enter into treaties with foreign countries; and, as a consequence of this rupture, the Shogunate, whose power had for some time been waning, completely collapsed. The Mikado was restored to imperial power, and at once entered upon a policy which has been consistently adhered to, and received with favour by the people generally, who had grown impatient of the restraint which environed them. That policy may be termed the Europeanization of the Empire; and in it we have the explanation of the Japan of to-day.

It is not surprising that the interest excited in England, with regard to a country which has experienced such remarkable changes, should be of the greatest—especially when it is remembered in how large a degree English influence has contributed to produce them. We may be certain, also, that the still further developments the future has in store, will be followed in our own country with a close attention. Equally natural is it that, in these days of so great fashion and facility for travelling, increasing numbers of English people should avail themselves of the opportunity of exploring a country so entirely unique, and so rich in its attractions of nature and of art. These circumstances have combined to call into existence a large number of books on Japan, from which any, who are unable to visit it in person, may obtain as good an idea as is possible by reading of the country, its people, and its customs. Indeed it is by no means easy for any writer now to fasten upon an aspect of the subject, in which he does not find himself forestalled. That, however, on which, so far as I understand, least has been written, is precisely that towards which my own main attention was directed from the time of my leaving England, and throughout the period of my visit to the country,—namely, the *religious* aspect. That the following pages must be very imperfect in the statement they supply, I am well aware; and that, despite my efforts to obtain trustworthy information, they will not prove free from inaccuracy or mistake is extremely probable. But I was induced to enter upon their preparation by a series of circumstances that appeared to favour such a task, and need not be specified here. For the material supplied to me, however, by one kind friend in particular, without whose assistance these articles would never have been attempted, I must express my special obligation. I would gladly refer to him by name, did I feel at liberty to do so without obtaining his permission, which I have not, at the time of writing, the opportunity of asking. Also, among the books I have consulted on the subject, I must acknowledge my great indebtedness to Messrs. Chamberlain and Mason's excellent *Handbook for Japan* (Murray, 1891); and to a copy of Dr. E. J. Eitel's *Lectures on Buddhism* (Trübner, 1871), given me by the author, at the close of a most interesting day spent under his guidance. The sketch Map of Japan is inserted by the kind permission of the "Guild of St. Paul."

November, 1893.

I. SHINTOISM.

When, in the sixth century of the Christian era, Buddhism was introduced into Japan from China, by way of Korea, the need was felt of some term by which the ancient indigenous religion of the country might be distinguished from the new importation. The term thus adopted was *Shinto*, or *Kami-no-michi*; the former being a Chinese word, and the latter its Japanese equivalent. The meaning of either, in English, is the "Way of the Genii, or Spirits [1]." It will, accordingly, be seen that the *word* "Shinto" has only been in use for some thirteen centuries, while the creed it designates claims to trace its origin from the remotest antiquity. Indeed, the investigation of Shintoism takes us back not merely to the earliest annals of Japanese history, but to the fabulous legends of a mythological period. The history of Japan is commonly

[1] This rendering seems preferable to the more usual "Way of the Gods." The term *Polytheism* is not, strictly speaking, applicable to Shinto.

reckoned to commence with the accession of the Emperor Jimmu Tenno, the date of which is given as February 11, 660 B.C.; and when, in 1889, the new Constitution was promulgated, the anniversary of this event was the day selected—the idea evidently being to confirm the popular belief in the continuity of the country's history. This Jimmu Tenno—accounted by the Japanese their first human sovereign—is supposed to have been descended from Ama-terasu, the sun-goddess, who was born from the left eye of Izanagi, the creator of Japan; and this it is that accounts for the semi-deification in which the Emperors of Japan have ever been held. It is, then, the countless heroes and demi-gods of the mythological age referred to—the children of Izanagi reigning over Japan, generation after generation, for many thousands of years— that are the chief objects of Shinto veneration; for while it is usual to speak of Shintoism as being a combination of ancestor-worship and nature-worship, it would seem that the latter of these elements was largely due to the contact of Japan with the Taouism of China, and with meta-physical Buddhism. Thus the essential principle of Shintoism, it will be seen, is closely akin to that filial piety, which forms so conspicuous a feature in the religious, political, and social life of China, and which—deserving as it is, in many ways, of respect and admiration—presents, when carried to excess, so vast a hindrance to development and progress.

"Shintoism," in the words of Diayoro Goh, Chancellor of the Japanese Consulate General in London, "originated in the worship offered by a barbarous people to the mythological persons of its own invention." To speak accurately, it is not so much a religion as patriotism exalted to the rank of a creed. It is a veneration of the country's heroes and benefactors of every age, legendary and historical, ancient and more recent; the spirits of these being appealed to for protection. Interwoven with this, its fundamental characteristic, and to a great extent obscuring it, is a worship of the personified forces of nature; expressing itself often in the most abject superstition, and, until lately, also in that grosser symbolism with which the religion of Ancient Egypt abounded. This latter feature was widely prevalent in Japan at the time that the country was first opened to foreigners; but after the Revolution in 1868, it was everywhere suppressed. It would appear that the personal cleanliness for which the Japanese, as a nation, are celebrated, had its origin in the idea of the purification of the body symbolizing the cleansing of the soul; and in a vague and hazy sort of way, Shintoism would seem to recognize a future state of bliss or misery, for which the present life is a period of probation. Practically, however, this is the only world with which Shintoism concerns itself; nor does it inculcate any laws of morality or conduct, conscience and the heart being accounted sufficient guides. It provides neither public worship, nor sermons; while its application is limited to subjects of the Mikado. "It is the least exacting of all religions." When this is once understood, there ceases to be anything surprising in the fact of two religions—of which Shintoism was one, and the other a creed so accommodating as Buddhism—running, side by side, for centuries in the same country, and being professed simultaneously by the same people, until the two were so closely interwoven that it became scarcely possible to distinguish their respective elements. In the eighteenth century an attempt was made to restore Shintoism to its primitive simplicity, and to mould it into a philosophical system which might minister to the higher aspirations of humanity. But the movement was a failure, and the Ryobu-Shinto, or "double religion,"—the combination, that is to say, of Shintoism and Buddhism—continued as before. It was only so lately as the year 1868 that any important change took place in the religious history of Japan. In that year, Shintoism—for reasons wholly political— was adopted as the State, or "established" religion; Buddhism having always been the religion favoured by the Shogunate, and the ancient nobility whom the Shogun represented. Upon this, every temple was required to declare itself either Shinto or Buddhist, and to remove the emblems and ornaments peculiar to the discarded cult, whichever that might be. That no little excitement and dispute followed upon this proclamation, will be readily understood; especially when we bear in mind that, for several hundred years, Buddhist and Shinto clergy had taken their turns of officiating in the same buildings and at the same altars [1]. A grant of some £60,000 a year was made by the Government for the maintenance of the Shinto temples and shrines, which are said to number in all about 98,000, and to be dedicated to no less than 3,700 different Genii, or Kami. Already, however, Shintoism has lost the greater part of the importance into which it was brought at the time of the Revolution; and, apart from the fact that it is supported out of the imperial revenues, and that the presence of its principal officials is required at certain of the state functions, its general position has in no way improved. The people still practise

[1] One of the great temples at Shiba, Tokio, was burnt by the Buddhists to prevent its falling into the hands of the Shinto priests. It may be mentioned here, as an instance of the liberal feeling of the present (Shinto) government, that one of this same group of buildings was lent for the Church of England services, before St. Andrew's Church was built. It is the old nobility who have been throughout the uncompromising opponents of Christianity, and indeed of all change; and the most zealous supporters of Buddhism

the observances of both religions alike; the only difference being that, to effect this, they have now to visit two temples instead of one. A new-born child, for instance, is taken by its parents to both Shinto and Buddhist temples, for the purpose of solemn dedication. Another of the changes brought about is that, instead of all funerals being conducted by Buddhist priests, as was the case until 1868, the dead are now buried by either Shinto or Buddhist clergy, as the relatives may prefer. Of the many signs which indicate that Shintoism has well nigh run its course, not the least remarkable was the announcement made last year (1892) by the Government itself, to the effect that its rites were to be regarded as simply traditional and commemorative, and devoid of any real religious significance. The relief thus afforded to the minds and consciences of Christians in Japan was, as might be supposed, very great.

Of the various sects the *Zhikko*,—founded 1541 A.D.,—is, perhaps, the most influential. This sect—as indeed do Shintoists generally—recognizes one eternal absolute Deity, a being of infinite benevolence; and here—as in other heathen religions—we find vague references to a Trinity engaged in the work of Creation.

Despite the dissociation of the two religions, many of the Shinto temples still retain traces of the Buddhist influence. Of Shintoism proper the prevailing characteristic is a marked simplicity, which, however, is often found combined with great artistic beauty. Sometimes the shrine consists only of a rude altar, situated amid a grove of trees; but, even in the case of large temples with a complete group of buildings, the architecture is extremely plain, the material employed being unornamented white wood with a thatch of chamaecyparis. The entrance to the temple grounds is always through gateways, called *Torii*; these are made sometimes of stone, but more properly of wood, and consist of two unpainted tree-trunks, with another on the top and a horizontal beam beneath. Near the entrance are commonly found stone figures of dogs or lions, which are supposed to act as guardians. The principal shrine, or *Honsha*, is situated at the further end of the sacred enclosure, and is divided by a railing into an ante-room and an inner sanctuary. Within the sanctuary an altar is erected, on which, however, no images or adornments are seen, but simply offerings of rice, fruit, wine, &c. Above the altar, in a conspicuous position, a large mirror is generally placed; and in a box beneath are usually kept a sword, and a stone. These three,—the mirror, the sword, and the stone,—constitute the Japanese regalia, and they are all connected with the early legends. One of the traditions respecting the sacred mirror deserves quotation.

GROUP OF SHINTO PRIESTS WITH TORII.

[To face page 24

"When the time was come that Izanagi and his consort should return together to the celestial regions, he called his children together, bidding them dry their tears, and listen attentively to his last wishes. He then committed to them a disc of polished silver, bidding them each morning place themselves on their knees before it, and there see reflected on their countenances the impress of any evil passions deliberately indulged; and again each night carefully to examine themselves, that their last thoughts might be after the happiness of that higher world whither their parents had preceded them." The legend goes on to relate with what faithfulness "the children of Izanagi, and afterwards their descendants, carried out these injunctions; erecting an altar of wood to receive the sacred mirror, and placing upon it vases and flowers,—and how, as a reward for their obedience and devotion, they became in their turn, the spirits of good, the undying Kami [1]."

Another of the most common of the Shinto emblems is a slim wand of unpainted wood, called *Gohei*, to which strips of white paper—originally they were of cloth—are attached. These are thought to attract the deities, and are held in great veneration.

Leaving the principal shrine, and proceeding to make the tour of the grounds, the visitor comes, in

[1] Eden's *Japan, Historical and Descriptive.*

turn, to the buildings where the business arrangements of the temple are transacted, and where the priests, in some cases, reside; to smaller shrines and oratories; to cisterns for the purpose of ceremonial ablution, &c. Sometimes, also, at the more important temples is found a long covered platform, called the *Kagura-do*, where, on festivals and special occasions, a number of girls—those I saw at Nara were still quite children—perform the *Kagura*, or sacred dance. The dancing is in honour of the divinity to whom the temple is dedicated; and commemorates a supposed incident of the mythological period. In the grounds of Shinto and Buddhist temples alike are frequently found numerous stone-lanterns, erected by way of votive offerings, and lighted on any great occasions.

It has already been remarked that Shintoism has nothing corresponding to our public worship; but every morning and evening the priests—whose office seems held in no particular sanctity, and who are at liberty, at any time, to adopt a more secular calling—perform a service before the altar, vested in white dresses, somewhat resembling albs and confined at the waist by a girdle. The service consists of the presentation of offerings and of the recital of various invocations, chiefly laudatory. The devotions of the people are remarkable for their brevity and simplicity. The worshipper, on arriving at the shrine, rings a bell, or sounds a gong, to engage the attention of the deity he desires to invoke; throws a coin of the smallest possible value on to the matting within the sanctuary rails; makes one or two prostrations; and then, clapping his hands, to intimate to his patron that his business with him is over, retires— it not being considered necessary to give to the petition any verbal expression. The making of pilgrimages, however, still occupies a prominent place in the Shinto system, and though of late years the number of pilgrims has considerably decreased, long journeys are still undertaken to the great temple of the sun-goddess at Ise—the "Mecca of Japan,"—and other celebrated shrines. The chief object of the pilgrimage is the purchase of *O-harai*, or sacred charms, which can only be obtained on the spot. These, when brought home, are placed on the *Kamidana*, or god-shelf—a miniature temple of wood, found in every Shinto house, to which are attached the names of various patron deities, and the monumental tablets of the family. His purchase of the O-harai completed, the pilgrim betakes himself to the enjoyment of the various shows and other amusements provided for him in the neighbourhood of the temple.

To conclude this brief sketch of Shintoism. Such influence as the cult still possesses may be attributed to the superstition of the poor and illiterate; and to a reluctance, on the part of the more educated, to break with so venerable a past. The latter, however, though they continue to conform to them, do not regard its observances seriously; while the importance attached to them by the State is, as we have seen, wholly political. In the words of Diayoro Goh, spoken in the course of a lecture delivered in London two or three years since: "Shintoism, being so restricted in its sphere, offers little obstacle to the introduction of another religion,"—provided, as he added, that the veneration of the Mikado, which has always formed the fundamental feature of Japanese government, is not interfered with. The truth of this statement has already been abundantly exemplified in the position which Buddhism for so many centuries held in the religious life of Japan. In the same way, when, three hundred years ago, Christianity was introduced into the country by the Portuguese, it was largely owing to the attitude which some of the missionaries adopted towards these national rites, that the complications arose, which eventually led to the expulsion of foreigners, and the persecution of Christians. And surely, when we think of it, it is not strange that an intense jealousy should be exhibited on behalf of observances and ceremonies, traceable back to such remote antiquity, and so intimately bound up with the whole political and social life of the nation. It is, indeed, highly probable that, in the great changes Japan is undergoing, she will find other methods of cherishing the continuity of her, in many ways, illustrious past. But meanwhile, Christians in Japan may rejoice that they are permitted, with a quiet conscience, to manifest a respectful regard for a system that is by no means destitute of praiseworthy features.

II. BUDDHISM.

It is quite possible that to some of the readers of these pages the very name of Shintoism was unknown; whereas all will have heard and read at least something of Buddhism, one of the four most prevalent religions of the world, and claiming at the present day considerably more than four hundred millions of adherents[1]. At the same time, our inquiry into Buddhism cannot be comprised within such narrow limits as sufficed for our examination of the indigenous religion of Japan; the subject being one of the vastest dimensions. Perhaps, then, it may be better if, at the outset, I allude to some of the literature, published within the last few years, which has been most instrumental in attracting attention, both in England and America, to the subject. Nor, in this connexion, can all

---

[1] Even an approximate total is difficult to calculate. At the lowest estimate we have a number considerably exceeding the whole mass of Christians. But it is important to bear in mind that in China, *which supplies more than three-fourths of the total number*, both Taouism and Confucianism are professed in conjunction with Buddhism. See Rhys Davids' *Buddhism*, chap. I (S.P.C.K.).

reference be omitted to the writings of the late Madame Blavatsky, Mr. Sinnett, and their school; though I refer to them only in order to caution my readers against forming from them any estimate of Buddhism. The only literature, as far as I know, that has appeared in England from what claims to be an enthusiastic Buddhist stand-point, these writings are, I believe, calculated to convey a curiously erroneous idea of the great system with which we are now concerned, to any who would turn for information to them exclusively. This, indeed, becomes obvious when it is understood that the Buddhism, of which these books profess to treat, is not the Buddhism of history and the sacred books, not the Buddhism which forms the popular religion of hundreds of millions of Asiatics at the present day, but an "esoteric" Buddhism, a knowledge of which, it is admitted, is confined to a comparative few, even in the country where it is said to be most prevalent[1]. In short, the "esoteric Buddhism" of Mr. Sinnett and his friends would seem to be scarcely, if at all, distinguishable from the movement which has recently acquired a brief notoriety in England under the name of Theosophy; and with this, Buddhism proper—i.e. the historical, popular Buddhism with which we have to do—can hardly be said to have anything in common.

[1] Thibet.

With the book, however, which probably more than any other work of the day has been the means of drawing the attention of English-speaking people to Buddhism, we cannot deal in so summary a fashion. For in Sir Edwin Arnold's poem, *The Light of Asia*, we have a work which is simply a rendering of the life of Buddha, in general accordance with the received traditions, and one, moreover, which has met with a cordial welcome at the hands of Buddhists. Nor can it be questioned that the book is a production of great power, or that it appeals altogether to a very different class of readers from that likely to be influenced by the *Occult World*, or *Isis Unveiled*.

It is indeed, the great beauty of its poetry, and the book's consequent popularity, that only make the more necessary a reference which must to some extent take the form of a protest. To put it briefly, the case is this:—Men and women have risen from a perusal of the *Light of Asia* with a sense of damage done to their Christian faith, and with a feeling—confused, perhaps, but not the less real—that in Gautama Buddha they have been confronted with a formidable rival to Jesus Christ. How far the poem is responsible for this result we will not attempt to determine; and that such was no part of the author's intention we may readily believe. But that the minds of not a few have been perplexed and disturbed by the reading of this book is a certain fact; making it neither surprising nor regrettable that its publication should have been followed by works on the subject, written from an emphatically Christian point of view. To the fullest and ablest of these,—the Rev. S. H. Kellogg's *The Light of Asia and the Light of the World: a Comparison of the Legend, the Doctrine and the Ethics of the Buddha, with the Story, the Doctrine and the Ethics of Christ* (Macmillan, 1885),—I would refer those desirous of investigating fully the points at issue; contenting myself now with a few brief observations.

It is, then, important to bear in mind that Sir E. Arnold's poem is written in the person, and from the stand-point of an imaginary Buddhist. This is indicated plainly on the title-page, in the preface, and in the course of the poem itself; and when the book comes to be read by the light of this explanation, a limitation is cast about much of its more startling language. To take, for instance, such expressions as "Our Lord," "Saviour," "come to save the world," constantly assigned to Buddha in the course of the poem. However accustomed Christians may be to associate such terms with One only, and however pained they may feel at their being referred, under any circumstances and with any restrictions, to another, still it is obvious that their use becomes less open to objection, when placed in the mouth of a disciple, singing the praise of his Master,—and that Master, one who, it can hardly be disputed, wrought no mean work of deliverance on the earth. Far less admitting of satisfactory explanation are passages in the book in which we find transferred to Buddha and Buddhism ideas and language distinctively Christian; the solemn saying of Simeon to the Holy Mother, "A sword shall pierce through thine own soul also," and the still more solemn, "It is finished" of the Cross, being made to supply particularly distressing instances of such treatment [1].

Or once again: but what I would say now has already been urged by Dr. Eitel, in words which I cannot do better than quote. "I believe," he says, "it would be unjust to pick out any of those queer and childish sayings with which the Buddhist Scriptures and especially popular Buddhist books abound, and to lead people to imagine that Buddhism is little better than a string of nonsense. It is even doubtful whether the earliest Buddhist texts contained such statements at all; for, unlike our Bible, the Buddhist canon has undergone wholesale textual alterations ... As to the popular literature of Buddhism, and its absurdities, we might as well collect those little pamphlets on dreams, on sorcery, on lucky and unlucky days, on the lives and miracles of saints, which circulate among Roman Catholic peasants,—but would that

[1] *Light of Asia*, i. 142, and vi. 688.

give us a true picture of Roman Catholicism? Thus it is with Buddhism [1]." In other words, Dr. Eitel would urge that in order to deal fairly with such a subject, we must try to distinguish the essence of the thing itself from the abuses and follies that may, from time to time, have gathered round it; and this, it is to be feared, has not always been done by English writers, in treating of Buddhism.

For the sake of clearness, we may next proceed to trace a brief outline of the life of Buddha, according to the belief of Buddhists generally, and stripped of such legends and superstitions as find no credence with the more educated and intellectual. It is true that a doubt has sometimes been expressed as to the existence of Gautama Buddha at all; while even so eminent an authority as Mr. Spence Hardy declares his conviction that, owing to the lack of really authentic information, "it is impossible to rely implicitly on any single statement made in relation to him [2]." But even supposing the Buddha of the commonly-received traditions to be, whether in part or in entirety, a mere creation of Indian thought, the case undergoes no vital alteration; seeing that it is with the religion of Buddhism that we are mainly concerned, and only in quite a subordinate degree with the

[1] *Lectures on Buddhism*, pp. 62-3.
[2] *Legends and Theories of the Buddhists*, p. 187.

person of its supposed founder. The point is one that deserves careful attention, suggesting as it does at once the essential difference between Buddhism and Christianity, and the immeasurable distance which divides the two. For of Christianity it is no exaggeration to say that upon the truth of the received accounts of its Founder's Life and Person its whole position absolutely depends; whereas, could it be proved that Gautama never even lived, the system associated with his name would suffer no material loss,—and this, because in Buddha we are invited to contemplate only a teacher and a guide, one who would have men seek purification and deliverance by the same means as he himself needed to employ, and one who never claimed to be more than human. Most persons, however, will prefer to accept as, in the main, historically correct the commonly accepted outline of the life of Buddha which may thus be given:—

The reputed founder of Buddhism was one Siddhartha, known in later life as Gautama, and later still, by the title of Buddha, or the "Enlightened One." Siddhartha was a prince of the Sakya tribe, whose territories were situated some hundred miles north-east of the city of Benares. Hence he is often spoken of under the name of *Sakya-muni,* or the "Sakya sage." As regards his date, widely different opinions are held; sometimes it is placed as early as the tenth, and sometimes as late as the third century B.C. The most competent authorities, however, agree in following the Buddhists of Ceylon, and take 543 B.C. as the date of his death [1]. His father's name was Suddhodana; his mother was called Maia. Of the earlier years of Siddhartha's life we have little information that is at all to be relied on; but his early manhood appears to have been spent amid the luxury and self-indulgence customary with Oriental princes. Gautama, however, was a man of great benevolence, and we are told that, while still quite young, he pondered deeply on the mystery of the pain and suffering which held the human race in bondage. Presently, becoming dissatisfied with his own life of ease and pleasure, he made the "Great Renunciation"; turning his back, at the age of thirty, on wife and parents, home and wealth. After spending some years in travel, he retired to the forest, where he attached himself to a little band of ascetics, and practised severe forms of discipline and self-mortification; hoping thus to discover the secret of release from suffering. But meeting with no success, and still fast bound by the trammels of ignorance, he betook himself to contemplation; until one day, as he was seated beneath the Bo-

---

[1] Prof. Max Müller, however (*Hibbert Lectures*, 1878, p. 134 note), gives weighty reasons for regarding 477 B.C. as the year of Buddha's death.

tree,—henceforth to be accounted sacred [1]— the struggles of his soul prevailed, and he passed out of darkness into light. He was now Buddha, He who Knew, the Enlightened. The four truths to the knowledge of which Gautama thus attained, and which form the very foundation of the Buddhist doctrine, are these :—(i) That man is born to suffering, both mental and physical: he experiences it himself, he inflicts it upon others ; (ii) that this suffering is occasioned by desire ; (iii) that the condition of suffering in which man finds himself admits of amelioration and relief ; (iv) the way of release, and the attainment to Nirvana.

Here we must pause to make the inquiry, What is meant by *Nirvana*,—the goal of the Buddhist's hope and aim? Literally, the word means "extinction"; and hence it has often come to be regarded as a mere synonym for annihilation. The variety of opinions held by European scholars as to its meaning is, there is little doubt, due to the fact that Buddhists themselves are by no means agreed as to its precise significance. Is Nirvana a state of consciousness or unconsciousness? Is the personality perpetuated, or is the *ego* absorbed,— i.e. into Buddha? Such questions are differently answered by the different schools. Concerning the nature of Nirvana, Buddha himself, in his

---

[1] " The Buddhists look upon the Bo-tree as most Christians have looked upon the Cross."—Rhys Davids' *Buddhism*, p. 37 note.

DAIBUTSU AT KAMAKURA.

agnosticism, would seem to have been almost wholly silent. He appears to have simply taught that by the suppression and "extinction" of the natural passions and desires—anger, avarice, sorrow, and the like [1]—it was possible even here to enter upon a state of tranquillity, rest, and peace, which should attain hereafter to more perfect fulfilment. Of the various meanings attached to Nirvana by the different Buddhist sects, one extreme makes it scarcely distinguishable from complete annihilation, while the opposite extreme introduces us to the doctrine of the Paradise of the West, the Pure Land presided over by Amitabha Buddha, the abode of perfect happiness and delight. This remarkable development of Buddhism will claim our attention later [2].

[1] It is, no doubt, owing largely to the influence of Buddhism that the passion of *anger* is almost unknown in Japan. In the same way, a Japanese, though the heart were well-nigh breaking, would consider it a most unworthy thing to let his grief betray itself.

[2] Miss Isabella Bird (Mrs. Bishop), authoress of *Unbeaten Tracks in Japan*, well describes the impression produced on the spectator by the Daibutsus, or colossal images of Buddha, so common in Japan :—" He is not sleeping, he is not waking, he is not acting, he is not thinking, his consciousness is doubtful; he exists,—that is all; his work is done, a hazy beatitude, a negation remain. This is the Nirvana in which the devout Buddhist may aspire to participate."

The Daibutsu at Kamakura, of which an illustration is given opposite, is one of the largest in Japan. It is fifty feet high, and, as a work of art, is without a rival. The boss protruding from the forehead is supposed to represent a jewel, and to symbolize Illumination.

To return. After his enlightenment, it is said that Gautama was seized by the temptation to enter at once into Nirvana, without proclaiming his doctrine to the world. But putting the temptation from him, he began his ministry by announcing the tidings of release to the companions of his ascetic life, who, after scoffing for awhile, were at length convinced. In the course of this, his first sermon, Buddha proceeded to enunciate the eight steps on the path which leads to Nirvana:—(i) Right faith, (ii) right resolution, (iii) right speech, (iv) right action, (v) right living, (vi) right effort, (vii) right thought, (viii) right self-concentration. As time went on, Gautama began to gather round him a number of disciples, who became his constant companions. Part of each year he spent in rest and retirement; teaching and training his disciples, and receiving such as, attracted by his growing reputation, sought him out. The remaining months he occupied in travelling from place to place, proclaiming the good news of deliverance in the towns and villages through which he passed. Soon we find him establishing a Society or Brotherhood; the members of which severed their connexion with all worldly things, handed over their property to the Order, adopted the tonsure and a distinctive dress, and, following the Master's doctrine with strictness themselves, devoted their lives to its propagation. Any member, however, was at liberty to leave the Brotherhood, should he wish to do so. It is noticeable that Buddha's earliest followers were chiefly drawn—not, as in the case of a Greater than he, from the ranks of the poor and simple—but from the upper classes. Indeed, Gautama seems to have regarded the weak and ignorant as incapable of receiving his teaching. Children are hardly mentioned in the early Buddhist writings; and with regard to women, it was only with great reluctance that Sakya-muni eventually consented to the formation of a Sisterhood, the members of which were, as far as possible, to observe the same rules as the men—together with several additional ones, chiefly concerned with their subjection to the Brethren. In the same way, it is still the teaching of Buddhism that it should be a woman's highest aspiration to be reborn as a man, in a future state of existence. When, however, the two Orders—for men and for women—had been formed, there still remained a large number of either sex, who, without leaving their places in the world, were desirous of being reckoned among Buddha's followers. These were admitted as lay-adherents, one of their chief obligations being to contribute to the maintenance of the Brethren.

Having exercised his public ministry for forty years—without, as would appear, encountering any great opposition—and having committed his work to the Brotherhood, to carry on after his decease,

Buddha died, aged about eighty, and was buried with great pomp. It is recorded that, as the time of his departure drew nigh, he replied to his disciples' expressions of apprehension and sorrow, by saying that when he should no longer be with them in person, he would still be present with them in his sayings, in his doctrine. Another point on which he laid great stress before his death was that the Brotherhood should regularly assemble in convocation. Hence it came about that from very early times, the declaration, "I seek refuge in Buddha, Dharma (the Law), Samgha (the Brotherhood)," was adopted as the formula which any one, desirous of becoming a Buddhist, was required to profess. And it is the Trinity thus formed, which, represented to-day by the three great images above the altar of many a Buddhist temple, has its multitude of ignorant worshippers, who doubt not that three several divinities are the objects of their adoration and their prayer.

Such, then, as would appear, was the origin of Buddhism. Strictly speaking, and apart from its later developments, Buddhism is a religion which knows no God, which attaches no value to prayer, which has no place for a priesthood. Nowhere, perhaps, is its agnosticism more conspicuous than in the five main prohibitions, which are addressed alike to clergy and laity. The *first* of these forbids the taking of life,—human life chiefly, but other life as well; the *second* is against theft, whether by force or fraud; the *third* is against falsehood; the *fourth* forbids impurity, in act, word, or thought; the *fifth* requires abstinence from all intoxicants. The whole idea of GOD, it will be noticed, is entirely absent from the Buddhist Commandments. Infinitely removed above that other agnosticism, which cries, "Let us eat and drink, for to-morrow we die," Buddhism starts with the idea of the entire abnegation of self. But a self-denial that is undertaken, not for God, and in God for man, but merely to secure one's own peace and well-being—what is this but selfishness after all? Enjoining a rule of life that is essentially negative—the natural product of that blank despair of the world and of human nature which led to the Great Renunciation—Buddhism, as a religious system, has yielded but scanty fruits of positive holiness, of active benevolence. And yet,—wholly inadequate as such a system as this, even at its purest and best, must be to meet the needs of humanity,—false and even debased as are sometimes its teachings,—the one great message that Buddhism proclaims is a message of undeniable, if most imperfect, truth: the truth that would have man cultivate self-reliance, and attain to self-deliverance by means of self-control. "Work out your own salvation" is the injunction of Christianity. "By one's self," taught Sakya-muni, "the evil is one; by one's self must come remedy and release." So far the two systems are at one; the difference between them lies in the fact that the one places in our hands those supernatural weapons which alone make real victory possible, and that these the other knows not how to supply.

Hitherto, we have made no reference to the relation of Buddhism to Brahmanism. And yet we can no more hope to understand the work of Sakya-muni, without observing its connexion with Brahmanism, than we could afford to omit all mention of the Jewish Law and of Jewish Pharisaism, in speaking of the liberation wrought by our Lord Jesus Christ. The work and doctrine of Gautama Buddha,—with their mean between an ascetic severity, on the one hand, and a licentious self-indulgence on the other—their disregard of caste distinctions—their rejection of burdensome and profitless traditions—may be said to bear to the heavy yoke of Brahmanism a relation not dissimilar to that which freedom has to bondage. Laying hold of that which was ready to his hand, if so be he might mould and purify it, Buddha was a liberator and reformer in respect to what had gone before. Let us take, for example, the doctrine of metempsychosis, or, as it is commonly called, the "transmigration of souls." No doubt, there is a great deal connected with this doctrine in the Buddhist books that cannot but appear to us puerile and shocking; but still, we do not well, we do not justly, if, as do so many, we fasten such strange fancies on Buddha, or on Buddhism, as though it were from these that they sprang. So far from Sakya-muni being the originator of the theory of transmigration, a belief in it had, for centuries previously, been almost universal throughout the East; and his doctrine of Nirvana supplied an antidote to the belief in a practically interminable series of metempsychoses current at the time. With the theory of transmigration accepted on all sides, Buddha seems to have made use of it to the extent that he did, as affording a convenient solution of the difficulty presented by the unequal distribution of happiness in this life, and the absence of any satisfactory exercise of justice in the way of reward or punishment.

That the doctrine of metempsychosis should have been applied by Buddhists to their great Master himself, is only what we should expect to find. Gautama is accredited by Buddhists with some five hundred previous existences, in the course of which he passed through numerous stages of vegetable, animal and human life, until at length he attained to the highest degree of manhood. Throughout the changing circumstances of his being, he is said to have exhibited a transcendent and ever-increasing unselfishness and charity, which culminated in his freely giving himself to be re-born as Buddha for the world's deliverance. And it is this belief, probably, which has been the most potent factor in exalting the Philosopher and the Guide to a height, which is scarcely, if at all, distinguishable from the Throne of God.

I may conclude this chapter by quoting a passage from the late Dean Stanley's *History of the Jewish Church*, where he is referring to Gautama Buddha: " It is difficult for those who believe the permanent elements of the Jewish and Christian religion to be universal and Divine not to hail these corresponding forms of truth and goodness elsewhere, or to recognize that the mere appearance of such saint-like and god-like characters in other parts of the earth, if not directly preparing the way for a greater manifestation, illustrates that manifestation by showing how mighty has been the witness borne to it even under circumstances of such discouragement, and even with effects inadequate to their grandeur [1]."

---

[1] *History of the Jewish Church*, Vol. iii. Lecture xlv.

III. BUDDHISM IN JAPAN.

IN the last Chapter we sketched in outline the life and teaching of Gautama Buddha; omitting the many fanciful legends that have gathered round his name, and confining ourselves to what would be accepted by Buddhists generally. Of the long period that divides the death of Sakya-muni from the introduction of Buddhism into Japan about 550 A.D., it is no part of our purpose to treat in detail. But enough must be said to connect in some intelligible way these two events.

After the death of Gautama, his disciples are said to have gathered together, and recited all that they remembered of his teaching, arranging it in three divisions. This was the origin of the sacred books known as the *Tripitaca*, i.e. the "three baskets," the "three receptacles." The first of these—consisting of sayings, aphorisms, parables, &c., attributed to Buddha, together with his first sermon addressed to the ascetics, (the "Wheel of the Law,")—is known as the *Sutra* or "Canon"; the second is called the *Vinaya* or "Book of Discipline"; and the third, the *Abhi-*

dharma, i.e. the "Book of Metaphysics," the "Further Doctrine." Of the three books, the Sutra, being mainly ethical, would have a more general application than the other two; while the Vinaya would be chiefly applicable to the Brotherhood, and the Abhidharma concerned with abstruse philosophical dissertations. The Tripitaca, of which the Buddhists of Ceylon are the custodians, are written in Pali, an early modification of Sanskrit, and the sacred language of Buddhism; and they are, undoubtedly, the oldest and purest of the numerous Buddhist scriptures. The Sutra, in particular, is believed to be a faithful record of the actual teaching of Gautama. At the same time, it must be remembered that for some centuries after Sakya-muni's death, there is no proof of the existence of any written Canon; the probability being that his teaching was, for the most part, transmitted orally from generation to generation, and that it underwent in the process considerable alteration and addition.

With regard to the history of Buddhism, from the time of its founder's death until the middle of the third century B.C., we are practically without information. It appears, however, that parties and schools were already beginning to be formed. But about 260 B.C., India, from being divided into a number of petty kingdoms, became almost wholly united under the rule of one Asoka. Asoka's grandfather—the founder of the empire that was soon to assume such vast proportions—had revenged himself for the contempt in which, for his low birth, he was held by the Brahmans, by patronizing Buddhism; and Asoka, in turn, bestowed upon it all possible support. He made Buddhism the state religion, founded an immense number of monasteries, and sent forth missionaries in all directions. China was one of the countries visited; while a mission to Ceylon, in which Mahendra, Asoka's own son, took a prominent part, resulted in the conversion of the whole island.

Shortly, however, after Asoka's death, his empire collapsed, and Buddhism never afterwards exerted the same influence in India; though it remained widely prevalent until the eighth century A.D., and it was not until four centuries later that it became practically extinct. The Brahmans now regained their former ascendency; declared Gautama to be an "avatar"—or incarnation—of their god Vishnu; proceeded to incorporate into their own creed some of the most popular features of the Buddhist system; and then entered upon a destruction of the monasteries, and a severe persecution of all Buddhists living in India. But, as in the history of the Christian Church, persecution only resulted in the Gospel being afforded a wider area, so was it now with Buddhism. "They that were scattered abroad went everywhere, preaching the word." Among other countries to which the doctrine of Sakya-muni penetrated was Cashmere, whose king, Kanishka, a contemporary of Christ, extended to it his enthusiastic support.

At this point was reached an important crisis in the history of Buddhism. Already controversies about discipline and various minor questions had called into existence several different schools; but now a breach occurred, of such magnitude and destined to prove so lasting in its results, as to often have suggested comparison with the schism between Western and Eastern Christendom. A council was held under king Kanishka, which the Ceylon Buddhists refused to recognize; and from that time Buddhism has been divided into two main branches, known as the *Mahayana* and *Hinayana*,—the "Greater and Lesser Vehicles." The division thus brought about became, to a great extent, a geographical one; the Hinayana having its home in Ceylon, and, somewhat less exclusively, in Burmah and Siam, while the schools of the Mahayana predominate in Cashmere, Thibet, China and Japan.

Let us glance, for a moment, at their respective characteristics. The Hinayana and the Mahayana, then, are the names given to two great systems, or "schools of thought," which offer to "carry" or "convey" their followers to the rest of Nirvana.

Of the two, the Hinayana, or Lesser Conveyance, presents a much closer resemblance to early Buddhism. The distinguishing features of the Hinayana may be declared to be its adherence to the strict morality of primitive Buddhism, its greater simplicity of worship, its smaller Canon of scripture, and the fact that it appeals rather to the comparatively few, to those, that is to say, who are able and willing to make the surrender it requires. Whereas, in the Mahayana, or Greater Vehicle, we see a system characterized by that increased ease and laxity, which too often accompany a season of repose and the cessation of the enthusiasm that attends the establishment of a new movement. The chief features of the Mahayana may be pronounced to be its less exacting standard of practical morality, its willingness to descend to the level of the multitude, its subtle metaphysical distinctions, its meditative inactivity, its elaborate ceremonial, and its more extensive Canon of scripture.

We are now, at last, in a position to examine the history of Japanese Buddhism. If an apology seems needed for the length of our digression, I can only say that it appeared to me necessary for any profitable treatment of our subject. We have already seen how, as early as 250 B.C., China was visited by Buddhist missionaries from India. These are said to have been eighteen in number;

and their effigies may be seen in many a Chinese temple, where they are held in great veneration. In the first century A.D., Buddhism in China began to receive imperial patronage; some of its books being about the same time translated into the language of the country. The spirit of accommodation and adaptation, which has always formed so conspicuous a feature of Buddhism, manifested itself now in an association with Taouism which has continued ever since.

552 A.D. is the date assigned to the introduction of Buddhism into Japan, by way of Korea. At first, it appears to have made little progress, until the diplomatic action of one of its clergy brought it into favour with the Court. Prostrating himself one day, before the little son of the Mikado, the priest declared that he recognized in him the re-incarnation of one of the disciples of Buddha, and one who was destined to effect a great spiritual work in Japan. The Mikado was prevailed upon to confide the boy's education to the Buddhist priests; with the result that, when he grew up, he supported their cause with such zeal as to cause him to be sometimes spoken of as the "Constantine of Japanese Buddhism." Shotoku Taishi—for such was his name—acted for some time as regent, but never himself ascended the throne.

There is no doubt that the progress of Buddhism in Japan was largely facilitated by the adoption of tactics, which had been successfully employed in dealing with the barbarous tribes of India, and—as we have just noticed,—with China also. Indeed, its readiness to adapt itself to the circumstances, instincts, and prejudices of the people, with whom it has to do, is, as has already been implied, one of the most powerful and most striking peculiarities of Buddhism. In Japan, the Shinto demi-gods were Buddhaized, and declared to be manifestations of Gautama; while practices borrowed from the ancient national creed were introduced into the Buddhist ceremonial. In the eighth century, we find orders issued for the erection of two temples and a pagoda in every province; until, about the twelfth century, the two religions became associated in the manner indicated in our first chapter,—Buddhist and Shinto clergy officiating by turns in the same buildings, and the Shinto temples becoming filled with images, alike of their own demi-gods, and of Buddha and his companions. This state of things continued until 1868, when the Shinto cult was chosen to receive the exclusive recognition of the State, many of the Buddhist monasteries at the same time suffering spoliation. Within the last few years, however, Buddhism has been making strenuous efforts to recover its former power and position, and there is little doubt that it still exerts a real influence in Japan; while the collapse of Shintoism is, as certainly, a matter of no distant time. At Tokio, the capital, where the number of temples is enormous, the proportion of Buddhist to Shinto is in the ratio of ten to one; and on several occasions during my stay in Japan I noticed handsome new Buddhist temples in course of erection, or old ones being redecorated and restored. On the other hand, numbers are closed, or falling to pieces, for want of funds to maintain them.

At the present time, there are some twelve or more *principal* Buddhist sects in Japan, several of these being subdivided. The distinction between the various schools is much more closely preserved than in China; and, at least in the larger cities, each sect will be found represented by a temple of its own. The difference between the schools consists not only in the varied attitudes adopted towards some controverted question, but frequently also in the degrees of importance attached to some point which is held by all in common. For, as cannot be too emphatically stated, Buddhism is a *many-sided* religion [1]. The following extract from Sir Monier Williams' *Buddhism*, for instance,

[1] This is scarcely less true of Christianity; and it *must* be true, in some measure, of every religious system which attempts to minister to the needs of beings, so differently constituted, and so dissimilarly circumstanced, as are the members of the human race. As we proceed in this chapter to refer to the various schools of Buddhism and their characteristics, we can hardly fail to have suggested to us, more than once, those different aspects of Christianity, which have been the occasion of all our "schools of thought," and, alas, of how many of our divisions!

draws attention to the variety of aspects, from which it may, and indeed needs to be regarded by the student.

"In different places and at different times, its teaching has become both negative and positive, agnostic and gnostic. It passes from apparent atheism and materialism to theism, polytheism, and spiritualism. It is, under one aspect, mere pessimism; under another, pure philanthropy; under another, monastic communion; under another, high morality; under another, a variety of materialistic philosophy; under another, simple demonology: under another, a mere farrago of superstitions, including necromancy, witchcraft, idolatry, and fetishism. In some form or other it may be held with almost any religion, and embraces something from almost every creed."

To the same effect writes Dr. Eitel in his *Lectures on Buddhism* (pp. 1–2): "Buddhism is a system of vast magnitude, for it comprises the earliest gropings after science throughout those various branches of knowledge which our Western nations have long been accustomed to divide for separate study. It embodies in one living structure grand and peculiar views of physical science, refined and subtle theorems on abstract metaphysics, an edifice of fanciful mysticism, a most elaborate and far-reaching system of practical morality, and finally a church organization as broad in its principles and as finely wrought in its most intricate network as any in the world."

It would hardly be worth while to attempt any detailed description of the many Buddhist sects represented in Japan. To observe the main characteristics of the principal ones, and their points of difference from one another, will be amply sufficient for our purpose. The greater number of the schools were introduced from China, but a few are Japanese developments.

Let us take, first of all, the schools of the Hinayana, or Minor Vehicle, which, as we should expect, is not extensively represented in Japan. The Hinayana is represented by four philosophical schools, in two of which the materialistic element predominates, and in the two other the idealistic; while eschatological questions afford further ground for difference. The points in dispute between these philosophical schools of Buddhism are altogether so subtle and abstruse as to be extremely difficult of comprehension to any not thoroughly versed in such distinctions. Of the four sects referred to, one, called the *Kusha*, has for its characteristic the fact that it bases its teaching on the Abhidharma Pitaca.

To the Minor Vehicle belongs the curious system known as the " Holy Path." This has been described as a " debtor and creditor account kept with divine justice." Much less common than in China, the system of the "Holy Path" is yet widely practised in Japan. Elaborate tables are drawn up, containing a list of all good and bad actions it is possible to perform, with the numbers added which each counts on the side of merit or demerit. The numbers range from one to a hundred, or even more; and the tables afford an insight into the relative importance in which all kinds of actions present themselves to the Oriental mind. He who would tread life's journey along the Holy Path must, at least, aim at setting off his bad deeds by a corresponding number of good acts of equal value. At the end of each year, the account is balanced, and the overplus or deficit is transferred to the succeeding one. That such a system is liable to the gravest abuse, especially in the case of the more ignorant, is obvious; though, when conscientiously practised, it need not be supposed to be unproductive of good [1].

At present we have made no mention of the *Madhyameka*, or Middle Vehicle, which, as its name implies, occupies an intermediate place between the Greater and Lesser Conveyances. A compromise between these two great systems, the Madhyameka may be said to be characterized by a marked moderation, i.e. between an excessive strictness, on the one hand, and a too great liberty on the other. But though it is thus a faithful

---

[1] Those who would investigate the subject further are referred to Alabaster's *The Modern Buddhist* (Trübner, 1870).

exponent of Sakya-muni's original doctrine, the Madhyameka has never attracted any extensive following. It is represented in Japan by the sect called the *Sanron*.

We pass on to examine the schools of the Greater Vehicle. In the same way that the Kusha sect regards as its chief authority the Abhidharma Pitaca, there are two schools belonging to the Greater Vehicle, which base their teaching on the Sutra and Vinaya Pitacas respectively. The *Kagon* make the parables and sayings of Buddha contained in the Sutra their especial study; while the *Ritzu*, as adhering to the more ascetic side of Buddhism, have for their favourite book the Vinaya, or " Discipline."

The *Dhyana* or *Zen* sect is a Chinese school with numerous sub-divisions. Its distinguishing feature is the prominence it assigns to the life of contemplation. Mysticism is represented by the *Shingon*, the Mantra school of India transferred through China to Japan; and also by the *Tendai*, so called from a mountain in China, where the head-quarters of the sect are situated. The temples of the Shingon may usually be recognized by the two guardian figures at the entrance, with open and shut mouths, suggesting the mystic syllable A-UM. A peculiarity of both of these sects is the use of the prayer-wheels and cylinders so common in Thibet.

An element of mysticism also pervades the influential *Hokkai* sect, a Japanese offshoot of the Tendai, founded in the thirteenth century by a priest named Nichiren, who is said to have been born supernaturally of a virgin mother. The Hokkai are most jealously attached to their own ritual, and to other observances peculiar to themselves; and, inheriting the disposition attributed to their founder, exhibit a narrowness and intolerance rarely met with in Japan. Their characteristic may be said to consist in an emotional fanaticism; and a visitor to one of their temples will generally find a number of devotees,—who thus remain engaged for hours at a time,—chanting the invocation of the sect, "Adoration to the Lotus of the Law," to a deafening accompaniment of drums.

Two sects only now remain, but these by no means the least interesting or least popular: the *Jodo* and the *Shin-Jodo* (i. e. the New-Jodo). The distinguishing features of these sects,—which also find a place in the system of the Hokkai,—are their acknowledgement of the need of external aid, and their doctrine of the Western Paradise, presided over by Amitabha Buddha. How marked a departure from the original teaching of Sakya-muni, as observed by us, these schools present is sufficiently obvious; nevertheless, it is alleged that the revelation of the Paradise in the West was first made by Buddha himself to one of his principal disciples. In the distant West is said to dwell one named Amida, or Amitabha, that is to say "Illimitable Light." Immortal himself, immortal also and freed from all the trammels of transmigration are the vast multitudes of men [1] who inhabit the boundless regions which he rules. In that "Pure Land [2]," that "Undefiled Ground," everything beautiful and enchanting has a place, neither is pain or sorrow known; and thither nought that is evil or that defileth can come. Whosoever would attain to this heavenly country must rely, most of all, on faithful invocation of the name of Amida; he having, as is recorded, made a vow that he would only accept Buddhahood on condition that salvation should be placed within reach of all sincerely desirous of achieving it. Such is the doctrine of the Western Paradise, some of the descriptions of which read almost like echoes of the last chapters of the Bible. Unknown to the Buddhism of Ceylon, Siam, and Burmah, it can be traced back as far as the second century A.D., when it was certainly known in Cashmere, though it was not until three centuries later that it began to spread widely over Northern Buddhism. But the whole question of its origin remains wrapped in obscurity. At the present day, the devotion to Amida is very widely

[1] For it is men only who inhabit this Celestial Region: women, worthy of attaining to it, have changed their sex.
[2] *Jodo* means the "Pure Land."

KIYOMIZU-DERA, KYOTO.

practised in Japan, and it is extremely popular. No doubt, the more educated and intellectual Buddhist, —and the distinction thus suggested needs constantly to be insisted on,—would explain the Paradise of the West as being a mere allegory, and regard Amitabha, as he was originally conceived to be, as merely an ideal personification of boundless light. But to the people generally the Undefiled Ground and its presiding deity are actual, literal, realities.

We have said that the two sects in which the doctrine of the Western Paradise appears in greatest prominence are called the Jodo and Shin-Jodo. The former of these is Chinese in origin, but was established in Japan about 1200 A.D. by a priest, Enko Daishi by name, who was also a member of the imperial family. The head-quarters of this sect are at Kyoto, where the magnificent monastery of Chion-in forms one of the principal sights of that most interesting of Japanese cities. But of all the temples of Japan, those of the New-Jodo (or *Monto*) sect are at once the most handsome, the most frequented, and the most attractive to the European traveller. Everything here, too, is of a dignified and stately character; there is a striking absence of the tawdry and the puerile. Founded in the year 1262, this sect is, at the present day, foremost in learning, influence, and activity. Another purely Japanese development, it is—owing to differences about "church government"—composed of two sub-divisions, the *Nishi-Hongwanji* and the *Higashi-Hongwanji*, or the Eastern and Western Divisions of the True Petition,—the reference being to the vow of Amida. In most of the larger towns, handsome temples of either branch are to be found, situated usually in the poorer districts.

It is in the temples of the Shin-Jodo that the remarkable similarity, of which every one has heard, between the Buddhist ceremonial and that of the Roman Church is most conspicuous. Nowhere, perhaps, did the resemblance in question,—to which I shall have occasion to refer again,—impress me more forcibly than it did in the New-Jodo temple at Nagasaki, at the first Buddhist service at which I was ever present. The day of our visit chanced to be the founder's anniversary, and from a raised lectern in the chancel, a venerable priest, of benign countenance,—wearing a rich vestment not unlike a dalmatic, and a cap resembling a biretta,—was recounting to a congregation, composed chiefly of women, old men, and children, the virtues of their deceased benefactor. Presently, the sermon came to an end, and the colloquial delivery of the discourse was changed for the monotone of a litany recitation: the people answering with ready response, and many of them employing the aid of their rosaries. The fragrance of incense filled the air; tapers and flowers adorned the altar, above which was the statue, not—as one entering by chance might almost have expected to see—of a Christian saint, but of some manifestation of Gautama Buddha. Despite, however, its elaborate ritual, the Shin-Jodo sect has been called the "Protestantism of Japan"; the reason being that it sanctions the marriage of its clergy, approves the reading of the scriptures in the "vulgar tongue," permits a wider freedom in respect to food and drink, and affords other indications of a "reforming spirit." The priesthood in this sect is, practically, a hereditary office.

In the *Great Indian Religions* of the late Mr. Bettany, there is given a summary of the Shin-Jodo Belief, in the words of one of its principal teachers. I will take the liberty of re-quoting it here. "Rejecting all religious austerities and other action, giving up all idea of self-power, we rely upon Amida Buddha with the whole heart for our salvation in the future life, which is the most important thing: believing that at the moment of putting our faith in Amida Buddha our salvation is settled. From that moment invocation of his name is observed as an expression of gratitude and thankfulness for Buddha's mercy. Moreover, being thankful for the reception of this doctrine from the founder and succeeding chief priests whose teachings were so benevolent, and as welcome as light in a dark night, we must also keep the laws which are fixed for our duty during our whole life." The mutual relation of faith and works is especially to be noticed; and indeed the strikingly *evangelical* character of the whole Confession.

Vast, however, as is the power attributed to Amitabha, and great as is the merit to be acquired by the invocation of his name, there is found in the temples in which he is worshipped an image which receives even more veneration than his. That colossal female effigy, with the many heads and countless hands, before which a number of votaries, composed largely of women, are kneeling in prayer, is meant to represent the mighty Avalokitesvara, or—to substitute for the Sanskrit the less formidable titles by which she is known in China and Japan,—the all-powerful Kwanyin or Kwannon. Here, again, we are confronted with a devotion the origin of which is wrapped in uncertainty, but which, closely connected with the doctrine of the Western Paradise, seems to have arisen some three centuries after the commencement of our era. At the present day, it is spread extensively over Thibet, Mongolia, China, and Japan; but it is unknown to the countries of Southern Buddhism. With regard to the meaning of this great image before us, Kwannon is commonly explained to be the reflex or spiritual son of Amitabha Buddha, sent by him to earth to preside on earth over the Buddhist faith, and appearing, at

STATUES OF KWANNON, SAN-JU-SAN-GEN-DO.

first in male and subsequently in female shape. But the probability is that the various personages, with whom Kwannon is supposed to be identified, had merely a fictitious existence; and that in her statues, we see simply an apotheosis of Mercy, an allegorical *Mater Misericordiae*, whose many eyes and hands are intended to signify the unremitting vigilance and the untiring energy with which she ministers to all sorrow and distress[1].

The island of Pootau, off Ning-po, in the Chusan Archipelago, is the great centre of Kwannon worship; the most popular of the many legends concerning her associating her with this locality, and offering an explanation of her thousand heads and hands more clumsy even than is the manner of such myths. The island belongs to the Buddhist priesthood, and is a great resort of pilgrims. In Japan, the shrines and statues of Kwannon are to be met with everywhere: many of her images being of enormous size, richly gilt and beautifully wrought. Sometimes the statues are kept concealed from view, either on account of alleged

[1] Avalokitesvara = "The Lord who looks down from heaven." The female form taking the place of the male is, no doubt, due to the idea of the woman's being supposed to be the more compassionate nature; just as, too often in the Christian Church, the Blessed Mother has, for a like reason, been made to encroach upon the prerogatives of her Divine Son. Instances are recorded of the Chinese, when conversing with Europeans, giving the name of *Kwanyin* to the statues of the Blessed Virgin in the Roman Churches. (Davis' *The Chinese*, chap. xiv.)

miraculous properties, or for some other reason of special sanctity. The highly-venerated image, for instance, at the Asakusa temple, Tokio, is never shown; it is only two inches high, and is accredited with supernatural qualities. But of all the shrines of Kwannon, it may be doubted whether the impression created by any is greater than by her temple of San-ju-san-gen-do at Kyoto, where no less than 33,333 images of the goddess may be seen. Of these a thousand are gilded statues, five feet in height, and ranged in tiers along a vast gallery. The remaining effigies are depicted on the foreheads, hands and nimbi of the larger ones. The temple and its contents originated in the votive offering of a Mikado of the twelfth century for recovery from sickness.

ALTAR OF SAN-JU-SAN GEN-DO.

IV. BUDDHISM AND CHRISTIANITY.

The Buddhist temples in Japan are for the most part built on a much grander and more elaborate scale than those belonging to the Shinto worship. The roofing is not of thatch, but of tiles; and instead of the torii, the entrance is through a *Sammon*, or two-storied gateway, in the recesses of which stand two huge figures of ferocious appearance. These are called *Nio*, and their office is to guard the sacred precincts from the approach of evil spirits. These images are commonly seen spotted all over with pellets of paper. "A worshipper writes his petition on paper, or better still, has it written for him by the priest, chews it to a pulp, and spits it at the divinity. If, having been well aimed, the paper sticks, it is a good omen." Passing through the Sammon, and proceeding in a straight direction—often between rows of votive stone-lanterns—the visitor soon arrives at the two largest buildings of the temple group. One of these is the *Hondo*, or main shrine; while the other may be either the Hall of the Founder of the particular sect to which the Temple belongs, or it may contain a colossal image of Amida, and be specially dedicated to his worship. Sometimes, again, this second building is known as the Refectory, from the spiritual nourishment supplied there in the form of sermons, for which the preacher takes as his text some passage of the Sutra, or, it may be, some saying of Confucius[1]. Removing our boots, which we leave at the foot of the wooden steps, we ascend to the Hondo, and, if need be, push aside the sliding-doors of paper-covered woodwork, which afford access to the building. Should no service chance to be in progress, a little company of priests, acolytes, &c., will probably be found, seated on the matting with which the floor is covered,—engaged in the perusal of book or newspaper, or chatting together over miniature cups of tea, and, if it be winter-time, spreading their hands to receive the grateful warmth of the *hibachi*[2]. Beside them, on the

---

[1] I have not thought it necessary in this little volume to introduce the subject of Confucianism. Even in China it is less a religion than a system of philosophy—political, social, moral. It may, however, be remarked that the writings of Confucius are highly esteemed in Japan, and that, in the past at any rate, they have had a considerable influence in forming the thought and character of its people. The ethics of Confucius being materialistic, i.e. concerned with the things of this present life, and the Buddhist ethics being mainly spiritualistic, the two mutually supplement each other. The great Confucian Temple at Yeddo was until 1868 the chief University of Japan. Now,—so entirely have the Western systems of education supplanted the teaching of the Chinese sage,—the building has been converted into a Museum. [2] Charcoal-brazier.

GUARDIAN NIO.

floor, is arranged a miscellaneous assortment of sacred pictures, leaflets, candles, incense-sticks, charms, and other articles; any of which may be purchased by a very modest expenditure. As we enter, we observe that several pairs of eyes are fastened on us in undisguised curiosity; but our low salutation is promptly responded to, if indeed it has not been anticipated, and one of the group will courteously come forward to supply us with any assistance or information we require. Before the railing, which encloses the sanctuary, two or three worshippers are kneeling in prayer; and these also examine us for a while with close attention. Or, it may be that at the time of our visit some religious function is proceeding. If so, the clergy with their servers are found within the chancel, clad in gorgeous yellow robes, and genuflecting now and again before the images which stand above the richly-vested altar. Outside the sanctuary rails, the congregation is assembled in greater or less numbers, according to the importance of the day. Around is a profusion of lights and flowers; while the air is fragrant with the fumes of incense. The prayers, which the officiating priest recites in monotone, are in Pali, a form of Sanskrit; and if an air of perfunctoriness pervades his devotions, let it be remembered that every day, month after month, and year after year, he may be found chanting these same litanies, of the significance of which he has but the vaguest idea. Not, however, that he is without belief in their efficacy; nay, it may be that his very ignorance of their meaning causes the words he utters to have, in his eyes, a transcendent value. Above the high altar, in seated posture on lotus-blossoms [1], are three colossal images, cunningly wrought and richly gilded, and bearing on their countenances an expression of placid repose. Perhaps, it is the *Triratna*, or Three Jewels, that these represent, the Trinity of Buddha, the Law, and the Order. Or, possibly, this is Buddha, in his triple forms of existence:— as Sakya-muni, the form under which he lived as man among men; as Amitabha, his metaphysical existence in Nirvana; as Avalokitesvara, his reflex in the world of forms, his spiritual son, generated to propagate the religion established by him during his earthly career. Or once again, these three images may portray the Buddhas of the Past, Present, and Future:—Gautama who *was*, the historic founder of Buddhism; Kwannon, or Avalokitesvara, the head of the present Buddhist hierarchy, the Buddha who *is*; and Maitreya, or

---

[1] "The only reason I can ascertain for the constant recurrence of the lotus in Buddhist art and ceremonial is the idea of its being the symbol of purity. Its scent and aspect are alike delightful, and though rooted in mud and slime it abhors all defilement. If, therefore, men would but take it as their model, they would escape all the contamination of this corrupt world. Every man, it is said, has a lotus in his bosom, which will blossom forth if he call in the assistance of Buddha." *Unbeaten Tracts in Japan,* Vol. i. p. 292.

PAGODA AT NIKKO.

[*To face page* 71.

Meroku, the deliverer yet *to come*, the rehabilitation of past Buddhas foretold by Sakya-muni. Now and again one may meet with a Buddhist of superior intellectual attainments, who would explain the acts of worship he offers to these images, as signifying merely reverence for Gautama's teaching; but to the multitude, as has been seen already, the images represent distinct and all-powerful deities. Indeed, the people are encouraged thus to regard them by their ecclesiastical superiors; it being one of the methods of Buddhism thus to adapt its teaching to the capacity of dense and ignorant minds. And thus it comes about that a religion, commencing with agnosticism, meets the "craving for divinity," so deeply implanted in the nature of our race, by passing into what is, practically, a deification of humanity.

Leaving the Hondo, we next proceed to explore the grounds and remaining buildings connected with the temple. This lofty *Pagoda*, for instance, several stories high, is erected over some holy relic, —perhaps the vitrified remains of the founder, after cremation. A little further on, we come to the *Rinzo*, or Revolving Library, containing an entire set of the Buddhist scriptures. As these consist altogether of some 6,700 or 6,800 large volumes, it is clearly impossible for any one person to read them all. This, however, need not be regretted seeing that whatever merit might be obtained by a complete perusal, is freely extended to all, who will take the trouble to make this huge stand revolve; the structure being so arranged that a single push is sufficient for the purpose! The Rinzo was an invention of a Chinese priest, and is said to date from the sixth century. Owing to their costliness they are rarely met with; and the only two I remember seeing were at Asakusa, Tokio, and at Ikegami, the head-quarters of the Hokkai sect. Elsewhere in the grounds we come upon the *Shoro*, or Great Bell,—used not for summoning the faithful, but for the purpose of invocation and worship;—the *Koro*, or Drum-tower; the *Emado*, or "Ex-voto" Shed, the walls of which are covered with pictures, charms, and other offerings; cisterns for the purpose of ceremonial purification; a printing and publishing department; and, perhaps, a grotto with ghastly representations of the sufferings endured in the Buddhist hells. Usually, too, to be found in the sacred precincts, is a specimen of the *Ficus religiosa*, or sacred tree, under which Sakya-muni attained his enlightenment. At the rear of the temple buildings are situated the priests' apartments,—often a quadrangle enclosed by a colonnade,—the reception-rooms of which are beautifully decorated with *kakemonos*. Here the visitor is sometimes invited to a light repast of tea, cake, and fruit; the priests waiting on him the while with the most

PLAN OF BUDDHIST TEMPLE AT IKEGAMI, NEAR TOKIO. (Head-quarters of the Hokké-ú or Nichiren sect.)

The path to the left from the Entrance Gate leads to the Main Temple; that to the right to the Founder's Hall. To the right of the plan are the Drum-tower and Pagoda. Behind the Main Temple is the Kitsuzo or Revolving Library; and in the lower left-hand corner of the picture is the Reliquary. The two small buildings in the foreground are the Belfry and the Enndo. In the background are the Priests' Apartments and Reception-rooms.

[To face page 72.

courteous attention. And here may I be permitted to say a word about the Buddhist priests of Japan as I found them? They are commonly spoken of as lazy and ignorant, mercenary and corrupt; and it is to be feared that with regard to many, especially of the lower orders of the clergy, this witness is true. But speaking of those with whom I came into direct contact—the priests, for the most part, attached to the more important temples— I feel bound to say, that the impression I formed of them was, on the whole, a distinctly favourable one. With countenances often indicating close spiritual application, they appeared to perform their sacred duties with reverence and attention; while of the disinterested kindness and hospitality I received at their hands, as well as of the courtesy and patience with which they replied to my numerous questions, I would speak in terms of grateful appreciation.

A visit to a Buddhist temple, however, can hardly fail to suggest to any, who are at all familiar with the observances of the Roman ritual, a comparison to which we have already referred,—I mean the striking resemblance between the Buddhist ceremonies and such as have found place in the Christian Church. The high-altar with its haloed statues, flowers, candelabra, and ever-burning lamps; the side-altars, similarly adorned, above one of which, it may be, is seen the image of Maia, the mother of Gautama, bearing her infant-son in her arms; the priests, tonsured, mitred, arrayed in their rich vestments, and attended by their acolytes; the people, bending low in adoration, or telling their rosaries as they pray; the tinkling of bells and the perfume of incense; the dim light of the sanctuary, and the monotonous chant, in the unknown tongue, of the litanies uplifted for living and for dead:—these are only some of the points of correspondence with Roman Catholic observances which meet us in almost every Buddhist temple. Indeed, to attempt to specify such resemblances in detail would prove a laborious task. But while the similarity to which I refer is far too close and remarkable to be accounted for by mere coincidence, its explanation is by no means easy. Some would solve the difficulty by referring to the unquestionable fact that many of the ceremonies practised in the Christian Church are adaptations of ancient heathen rites: a leading captive of captivity of which, as it seems to me, Christianity has far more reason to be proud than ashamed. But though the Buddhist observances are, without doubt, of considerable antiquity, this explanation cannot be said to be adequate to the requirements of the case. Far more satisfactory is the theory that ascribes the phenomenon to an early contact of China with some form of Christianity—probably Nestorianism—and to the readiness which Buddhism has ever exhibited to extend its influence

A BUDDHIST PRIEST.

[*To face page 75.*

by a conformity to other faiths. The problem, however, is one which we must, to a great extent, be satisfied to leave unsolved; the most eminent authorities in Orientalism having confessed themselves baffled. It is only the fact of the resemblance that admits of no dispute.

It is curious to notice the different effects produced by an observation of the Buddhist ceremonial on the minds of Roman Catholic missionaries upon their first arrival in the East. By some its likeness to their own ritual has been regarded as a manœuvre of Satan, designed for the hindrance of Christian truth; while others have regarded the resemblance with satisfaction, as calculated to diminish the difficulties of their work. Without entering further into this question, I may be allowed to express the conviction that an elaborate ceremonial forms at any rate no necessary factor of Christian work in Japan. So far from this being the case, I was informed, on no prejudiced authority, that, the breach once made with the old associations, converts are disposed to regard anything tending even remotely to suggest them as more of a hindrance than a help; and this view finds support in the large number of adherents gained by several of the Protestant Missions, with whom anything in the way of ceremonial is reduced to a minimum. On the other hand, must be remembered the very successful work accomplished in Japan, alike by the Roman and Orthodox Churches, whose combined total of some 65,000 adherents is more than double that of the various Protestant sects,—the Churches of England and America, with 4,000 members, not being included in this computation.

Hitherto, I have referred only to the resemblance outwardly existing between the ceremonies and observances of Christianity and Buddhism. But an extension of the comparison results in what is, at first sight, an even more startling similarity between incidents recorded of Gautama Buddha, and events in the life of Jesus Christ, as narrated in the Gospels. Thus, we are told that Gautama was born of a virgin mother; that angels appeared at his nativity; that an ancient seer prostrated himself before him, and saluted him as one come down from heaven; that, as a child, he confounded his teachers by the understanding he displayed, and the questions which he asked; that, assailed by the Evil One [1] with the keenest temptations,—including the offer of Sovereignty over all the world, if he would renounce his mission,—he yet emerged victorious from all; that once, being on a mountain, he was enveloped in a cloud of heavenly light; that he went down into hell; and that he ascended into heaven. Indeed, the Christian may be

---

[1] Buddhists believe in the existence of a personal wicked spirit, named Mara, whose object is to solicit men to evil.

pardoned if, for the moment, he feels completely staggered at all that he finds advanced on behalf of Sakya-muni; and if his perplexity only begins to give place to relief, when he discovers that there is absolutely no trace of such extraordinary coincidence in the early Buddhist writings, and that there is no reason for supposing that these alleged events in the life of Gautama were ever heard of until the Christian era was already several centuries old.

We have now, as far as our limits permit, made an examination of Buddhism with especial reference to Japan. But before leaving this part of our subject, I would humbly, but very earnestly, submit the question, Is there in Buddhism generally,—is there in Buddhism as it exists in Japan at the present day,—nothing upon which Christianity may profitably fasten, nothing to which Christianity may properly appeal? Is that great proclamation of Christian tact, which, eighteen centuries ago, the Apostle Paul delivered on the Areopagus at Athens, "Whom ye ignorantly worship, Him declare I unto you," one that cannot, more often than it does, find a place on the lips of our missionaries of to-day? Is the position a useless one to take, that both the faiths of Jesus Christ and of Buddha agree in this, that either has for its object the amelioration of man's lot, here and hereafter, and his release from the curse of suffering; only, as we believe, with this great difference, that the founder of Christianity was possessed of resources to which Sakya-muni laid no claim? These are questions which were constantly presenting themselves to my mind during my visit to Japan; but they are questions also which I heard asked more than once by men who had closely studied the whole subject and were deeply interested in mission work. But whatever the true answer to these questions be, of this we may be certain: that by no reckless denunciation of a creed, of the very elements of which the denouncer is content to be in ignorance, will any victory of Christ's Cross be achieved. Be the errors and shortcomings of Buddhism what they may,—and we must, to be honest, pronounce them in our judgment to be many and great,—it is, at least, a system of very great antiquity, in whose strength thousands of millions of our fellow-creatures have lived and died, both better and happier. Men cannot be expected lightly to abandon their allegiance to such a faith as this, nor would it be to their credit if they did; while in Christianity, even when faithfully represented, there is very much calculated to perplex and estrange one who has been trained in the tenets of Buddhism. Moreover, however little he may agree with them, the Buddhist holds that the religious convictions of others are entitled to respect, and that their feelings should never be wounded, if this can be avoided; it is only natural that he, in his turn, should be quickly alienated by unsympathetic treatment. I was told by an English resident of long standing that infidelity is largely on the increase in Japan, especially among the men of the upper and middle classes; and that among the causes of this was certainly to be reckoned the contemptuous and merely destructive attitude towards Buddhism, with which some—let us hope they are the very few—would think to serve the cause of Jesus Christ. "Depend upon it," it was said to me, "it is irreligion that commonly succeeds to the vacant place, not Christianity. Carlyle was right when he said, 'Better even to believe a lie than to believe nothing.'" And Buddhism is not all a lie!

"The perishing heathen." Many of us have been revolted by such expressions when heard at home. But it is only when one is living in the midst of the people of whom they are spoken, that it is possible to realize the full horror of their meaning. That men, women, and little children, who are distinguished by so many good qualities[1], and who—with, as we believe, such immeasurably inferior opportunities—present, in many points, so

[1] Cf. the following extract from the speech of the Bishop of Exeter at the Annual Meeting of the C.M.S. 1892:—"If you had been asked to sketch an ideal land, most suitable for Christian Missions, and when itself Christianized more suited for evangelistic work among the nations of the far East, what, I ask, would be the special characteristics of the land and people that you

favourable a contrast to ourselves, should be condemned to a future of hopeless and unending misery, for not believing that of which, it may be, they have not even heard, or heard only in crude,

would have desired? Perhaps, first, as Englishmen or Irishmen, you would have said, 'Give us islands, inseparably and for ever united, give us islands which can hold their sea-girt independence, and yet near enough to the mainland to exert influence there.' Such is Japan—the Land of the Rising Sun. 'Give us a hardy race, not untrained in war by land and sea; for a nation of soldiers, when won for Christ, fights best under the banner of the Cross—for we are of the Church militant here on earth: give us brave men;' and such are the descendants of the old Daimios and two-sworded Samurai of Japan. 'Give us an industrial race, not idlers nor loungers, enervated by a luxurious climate, but men who delight in toil, laborious husbandmen, persevering craftsmen, shrewd men of business;' and such are the Japanese agriculturists, who win two harvests a year from their grateful soil—such are the handicraftsmen there, whose work is the envy of Western lands; such are the merchants, who hold their own with us in commerce. 'Give us men of culture, with noble traditions, but not so wedded to the past that they will not grasp the present and salute the future;' and such are the quick-witted, myriad-minded Japanese, who, with a marvellous power of imitation, ever somehow contrive to engraft their own specialities upon those of Western lands. Witness their Constitution, their Parliament, their 30,000 schools in active operation; witness their museums and hospitals; witness their colleges and universities. 'But,' you would also have said, 'give us a race whose women are homespun and refined, courteous and winsome, not tottering on tortured feet, nor immured in zenanas and harems, but who freely mingle in social life, and adorn all they touch;' and such, without controversy, are the women of Japan. Above all, 'give us a reverent and a religious people, who yet are conscious that the religion of their fathers is unsatisfying and unreal, and who are therefore ready to welcome the Christ of God;' and such are the thoughtful races of Japan."

distorted statement—can any man *really* think this, who recognizes the providence of a Father of Love; nay, I will dare to say, of a Deity of bare Justice? And yet language thus fearfully misrepresenting the Faith of Christ is still used by some who are called by His name; and that it is used is known by the people of Japan[1].

But again. There is, I have observed, much in the scheme of Christianity calculated to prove a stumbling-block to those who have been educated in the doctrines of Buddhism. Let me proceed to state some of the difficulties that would be experienced, some of the objections that would be raised, by a Buddhist of a certain amount of intellectual capacity, when confronted with the claims of the Christian Faith.

Thus, (*a*) *the Bible.* "We are unable," the Buddhist would say, "to recognize in your Old and New Testaments an inspired revelation. Why should we accept your Scriptures, with all their alleged miracles and supernatural occurrences,

---

[1] See on this subject Study VI in the late Dean Plumptre's *The Spirits in Prison*. The Christian can scarcely doubt that Gautama has, long ere this, fallen at the feet of the Crucified,—knowing at last the Name whereby he has been saved,—and has heard from the Divine lips the gracious approval, waiting to be bestowed on all men of good-will, of whatever age, of whatever land, who have 'worked righteousness,' and have faithfully responded to whatever measure of light and opportunity has been accorded them by God.

when you reject ours? Besides, you are not agreed among yourselves as to inspiration, authenticity, translation, interpretation. Some of you, again, are for diffusing the Bible broadcast, others would keep it in the background. Again, the Christian doctrine of immortality appears to us entirely absent from the pages of the Old Testament; while even the Jews, 'God's chosen people,' refuse to see in the New Testament the fulfilment of the Old."

(b) *The Old Testament.* "We cannot regard the story of Creation, as given in the Book of Genesis, as anything more than a myth, containing a germ of truth. Neither can we accept, as historically true, the story of the temptation in the Garden of Eden. And yet, upon this is made to rest your whole theory of the Fall, of Original Sin, and of Christian Redemption. As for the history of the Jewish people, we can see in it nothing but one long story of cruelty and bloodshed; how can a Creator, a God of Love, be supposed to have permitted and approved such things?"

(c) *The Incarnation.* The whole doctrine of the Incarnation is full of difficulty to the mind of an Oriental; *not* because of its strangeness and novelty, but owing to his very familiarity with stories of miraculous birth in his own legends.

(d) *The Atonement.* "Why should Jehovah require the sacrifice of His own Son?" This is a difficulty that would present itself with especial force to the Buddhist; by whom all life is held sacred, and whom such texts as "Without shedding of blood there is no remission," fill with repugnance. The explanation offered by Buddhists themselves of the Christian doctrine of Atonement is, that its origin must be sought in the fact that, from the most ancient times, the idea of sacrifice, and of human sacrifice, has existed; and this explanation they go on to apply to the Holy Eucharist.

(e) *Eternal Punishment.* "How," it is asked, "is your doctrine of Everlasting Punishment consistent with that of the Remission of Sins? And how, on the other hand, is not your scheme of salvation ethically wrong, if it allows people, after sinning all their lives, to be forgiven on their death-beds, that so they may enter a Paradise, wherein good and bad alike have a place?"

(f) *Faith and Belief.* "What right have you to ask us to believe anything that does not accord with science and experience, when you have no better opportunities of knowing than we?"

(g) *Christian Ethics.* "Some of these—e.g. the doctrine of the Sermon on the Mount—we admit to be good; but they are not peculiar to Christianity—our own teaching is very similar. In other of your ethics, we see only an ignoble and selfish storing of treasure; it appears to us that a good action, done for the sake of reward or gain, must entirely lose its merit."

(*h*) *Missionary Work.* " *We* do not claim that our religion is the only way of salvation, but readily recognize the good points in other systems as well. *You*, on the contrary, appear to hold that there is no other way but your own; and indeed it is only on this supposition that we can understand the strenuous efforts which you make to bring us to abandon our religion for yours [1]."

It forms no part of my purpose to discuss these objections; which, let me add, are merely representative, and by no means exhaustive. With many of them we are already familiar at home; and the Japanese, I would mention, are fully aware of the unbelief prevalent in England, and well acquainted with its arguments. Indeed, few English people, it is probable, have any idea how closely their history and their literature are studied by nations living at the other side of the globe, who

---

[1] I may observe that the language, not only of the New Testament, but of the *Athanasian Creed*, was quoted to me in this connexion by a Buddhist priest in Japan. I endeavoured to point out to him,—how far convincingly I cannot say,—what at the present day at least is generally recognized amongst us; that for the Christian Church to warn her own children, in terms the most emphatic just because the most loving, against becoming entangled in the deadly errors prevalent at the time when the Creed was drawn up, is a thing wholly distinct from passing any sentence of eternal condemnation on, or, indeed, expressing any opinion as to the future state of, such as live and die without ever having been brought to a knowledge of the Faith. I added, of course, that any acquaintance with the claims of Christianity is a responsibility for which we believe all will have to give account.

are to them simply "the heathen." Some, again, of the above objections would seem to have been suggested by imperfect and distorted statements of Christian truth. I have thought it worth while to refer to them, in the hope that the fact of such questions being raised may serve to impress upon us these two important points:—(i) the need of missionaries, at the present day, being not only men of holy and devoted lives, but also fully equal in intellectual equipment and culture to our home clergy; and (ii) the fallacy of trusting to the circulation of the Bible, as an instrument of mission work, unless it be accompanied—or rather preceded—by the teaching of the living agent.

It must not, however, be imagined that the obstacles to the progress of the Gospel in Japan are wholly, or even mainly, of the character I have referred to. Another great hindrance is most unquestionably presented in the large number of competing sects and organizations, which, here as in other countries where mission work is being carried on, address the people in the name of Christianity. It is true that Buddhists themselves are divided into numerous sects and schools; but between these there can scarcely be said to be anything of party animosity and strife. It will, indeed, be heard with satisfaction that the feeling towards one another of the various Christian bodies in Japan is, speaking generally, free from bitterness; and that each would appear desirous of doing its own work, in the wide field before it, without interference with the efforts of others. "The feeling here," it was observed to me, "is nothing like so bad as it is at home[1]." And as in England bigotry and suspicion are steadily giving place to mutual toleration and respect, so may we hope that, both in our colonies and abroad, counsels of charity may more and more prevail. Still, at the best, so long as Romanists, Orthodox, Anglicans, and Sectarians adhere to the positions they at present occupy, so long must any real unity of action be impossible; neither can peace be sought by surrender or compromise of principle. But meanwhile there is, of course, a lamentable want of compactness among the converts—as a recent writer in the *Japan Mail*, remarked "they are more like scattered groups of soldiers than an army";—while the perplexity occasioned to those we are seeking to convince is terrible and great.

The following extract from Miss Bickersteth's recently-published *Japan as we saw it* (Sampson Low, 1893), draws an able contrast between the religious condition of Japan at the present day

---

[1] I doubt if the speaker, in his long absence from England, quite realized the extent to which, of the last few years, bitterness and intolerance have effaced themselves, at any rate within the limits of the Church of England; or was aware of the marked improvement that is exhibited amongst us in dealing with such matters of controversy as still remain.

and the position of Christianity in the time of St. Francis Xavier. "It was impossible not to be struck with the present complication of religious matters in the country as compared with the days of Xavier. Then, on the one side, there was the Buddhist-Shinto creed, undermined by no Western science, still powerful in its attraction for the popular mind, and presenting a more or less solid resistance to the foreign missionary; and, on the other, Christianity as represented by Roman Catholicism, imperfect truly, but without a rival in dogma or in ritual. Now the ranks of Buddhist-Shintoism are hopelessly broken; the superstition of its votaries is exposed by the strong light of modern science, and their enthusiasm too often quenched in the deeper darkness of atheism. Christianity, though present in much greater force than in the days of Xavier, is, alas, not proportionately stronger. The divisions of Christendom are nowhere more evident than in its foreign missions to an intellectual people like the Japanese. The Greek, the Roman, the Anglican churches, the endless "splits" of Nonconformity, must and do present to the Japanese mind a bewildering selection of possibilities in religious truth."

To refer to but one other hindrance to Christian progress in Japan—which, although the last mentioned, is by no means the least serious—I mean the estimate formed by the natives of the practical influence of the Christian religion upon English people and upon other nations professing it. Applying to Christianity the test of its results, they urge that it has, at any rate, only very partially succeeded. For instance, the Japanese comment upon the fact that numbers of Englishmen in Japan never attend the services of their Church; and that the lives of many of them display a flagrant disregard for the principles which should regulate the conduct of Christians. Without, however, denying either the justice of these charges, or the reasonableness of the mood which advances them, I think it may be urged with fairness that the influence of Christianity on us as a nation cannot rightly be estimated in this particular way. As a rule, the Englishman can scarcely be said to appear to advantage abroad. Too often he assumes an attitude of insolent superiority to the people whose guest he is; while the position in which our countrymen are placed in a country like Japan—coupled with the freedom from restraint, so much greater than at home—has, for reasons which we need not now enter into, its peculiar difficulties. Neither is it by any means certain that a Japanese, paying a short visit to England, will gather any just impression of what hold Christianity has on us as a people. In all probability the range of his observations will be very limited and superficial; his wanderings will be chiefly confined to the great thoroughfares of the principal cities; while the circle of his acquaintance will, it is likely, be equally restricted, and equally unrepresentative of English life. Not that, in saying this, we would seek to excuse ourselves, or deny that there is far more truth than we could wish, and than there ought to be, in the charges brought against us. We would merely submit that there is another side to the picture which ought not, in fairness, to be overlooked. Admitting as we must, for instance, the great prevalence of infidelity in our England of to-day, there is yet to be placed over against it,—and may I not add, drawing it out into the light?—the increased activity of the Church during this last half-century, the remarkable power she has exhibited of adapting herself to meet the needs of her times, the influence for good that she has not only been in the past, but remains at the present day, in the nation at large, and in thousands and thousands of English homes. "By their fruits ye shall know them": and Christianity must not and need not deprecate the application of that test to herself. Only, we would urge, that is not a fair judgment, which takes account only of what the Church of Jesus Christ has failed to do, without recognizing also all that, in the strength of her Divine Head, she has been permitted to accomplish.

V. CHRISTIANITY IN JAPAN.

I propose now to place before my readers some account of the various Missions at work in Japan. I am enabled to do this the better from having obtained, in the course of my visit, a useful table, compiled by the Rev. H. Loomis, of the American Bible Society, Yokohama, giving statistics of the different organizations up to the beginning of the year 1893. The plan adopted by Mr. Loomis is to arrange his statistics into three classes: (1) "Protestant Missions," (2) "Catholic Missions," and (3) "The Greek Church in Japan." Under the head of "Protestant Missions," are included the Church of England, the Episcopal Church of America, a large number of other American denominations, the Presbyterian Church of Scotland, the Swiss Evangelical Protestant Mission, the Society of Friends, U.S.A., Universalists, Unitarians and others; while under the head of "Catholic Missions" we find particulars of only one branch of the Holy Catholic Church—the Church of Rome. This is not the arrangement I should have made myself; but, as a matter of convenience, we will follow it more or less closely[1]. It is right to add that of the thirty "Protestant Missions" seven are grouped together under the title of the "Church of Christ in Japan," and work, it would appear, in general harmony on Presbyterian principles. In the same way, the American Episcopal Church, the Church of England—represented by both the Church Missionary Society and the Society for the Propagation of the Gospel —and the Mission of Wyckliffe College, Canada, are associated together; leaving some twenty sects working independently[2].

Before, however, proceeding to an examination of Mr. Loomis' table, we must briefly observe the past history of Christianity in Japan. This dates from the arrival of St. Francis Xavier in 1549, seven years after the country was discovered by the Portuguese. For some while the missionaries

---

[1] In the course of a letter appearing in *The Christian* of April 20, 1893, the Rev. H. Loomis writes, "Let the *forty thousand* Christians of Japan but dedicate themselves to the welfare of the country in all its relations, and the true new Japan will be founded." But Mr. Loomis himself has placed the total membership of "Protestant Missions" at 35,500, of the Orthodox Church at 20,300, and of the Roman Church at 44,800. To which sixty thousand of these does Mr. Loomis—presumably—refuse the title of "Christian"? and are we justified in acting thus towards any who believe in the Holy Trinity, and have accepted Jesus Christ as the Saviour of the World, Very God and Very Man?

[2] Even Mr. Loomis' list does not appear to be exhaustive! The "Plymouth Brethren," e.g., are certainly represented at Tokio.

were permitted to prosecute their work without molestation, and considerable progress was being effected. A deputation of native priests appealed to the Tycoon, but their remonstrances were unheeded. With thirty-five religious sects already represented in Japan, the country, he answered, might very well find room for a thirty-sixth religion, viz. Christianity. Presently, however, the Jesuits being followed by the Dominicans and Franciscans, mutual factions broke out; while, elated by their success, some of the missionaries began to adopt an attitude of high-handed intolerance and interference. For the first time in their history, the Japanese found themselves entangled in all the turmoil and animosity of religious strife. In 1587 the first persecution of the Christians took place, but apparently soon subsided. The warning, however, was disregarded; and the fatal policy of arrogance and oppression was still persisted in. Native priests were put to death; Buddhist monasteries were destroyed; the Inquisition was set up. In 1614 we find a Japanese embassy despatched to Rome, in order, so it is said, to make an act of submission to the spiritual supremacy of the Pope. Meanwhile the Dutch, jealous of the position that was being gained by the Portuguese traders, accused the Roman propagandists to the Japanese authorities of aiming at a territorial ascendency; and that intrigues were actually being carried on by the Jesuits for the overthrow of the Shogun there seems little doubt. In the massacre which ensued several thousand Christians were put to death. "Their unflinching devotion compels our admiration. One may search the grim history of early Christian martyrology without finding anything to surpass the heroism of the Roman Catholic Martyrs of Japan. Burnt on stakes made of crosses, torn limb from limb, buried alive, they yet refused to recant. We are told of one Jesuit priest, Christopher Ferreya, who, after enduring horrible tortures, was at length hung by his feet in such a way that his head was buried in a hole in the ground from which air and light were excluded. His right-hand was left loose that he might make the sign of recantation. He hung for four hours, and then made the sign; whereupon, with a rare refinement of cruelty, he was appointed the president of the tribunal before which Christians were brought for condemnation. Then, after a lull, in 1637 thousands of Christians rose in armed rebellion. After two months they were forced to surrender, and 37,000 were slaughtered. Stern decrees were then issued, forbidding the admission of any foreign vessel; an exception being made in favour of the Chinese and Dutch. For more than two hundred years, notice-boards stood beside highways, ferries, and mountain-passes, containing, among other prohibitions, the following:

—' So long as the sun shall warm the earth, let no Christian be so bold as to come to Japan; and let all know that the King of Spain himself, or the Christians' God, or the great God of all, if he violate this commandment, shall pay for it with his head.' For centuries the name ' Christian ' would blanch the cheek and pale the lip. Christianity was remembered only as an awful scar on the national annals. But in the Southern Island the smouldering fire was never quite extinguished; while, as recently as 1829, six men and an old woman were crucified at Osaka [1]."

At the time of the closing of the country to foreigners, an exception was made of the one port of Nagasaki, the scene of the final great massacre, when thousands of native Christians were hurled from a rocky islet into the sea. Here, however, as has been already mentioned, the Dutch were the only Europeans permitted to trade; they being closely confined to the small island of Deshima. In addition to having pay a heavy rental, they were subjected to the closest espionage, not being suffered, under any circumstances, to pass beyond the narrow limits assigned to them. Several times in each year they were summoned before the authorities, and required to tread under foot the Crucifix, and other symbols of the Catholic

---

[1] The above is an abridgement of a passage in the *Conquests of the Cross* (Messrs. Cassell & Co.).

Faith. Several of the trampling-boards employed on these occasions are still to be seen at the Ueno Museum, Tokio. The Dutch, it would appear, quieted any qualms of conscience by regarding their action as amounting to an abnegation, not of Christianity, but of Romanism. It was not until thirty years ago that intercourse between Japan and other nations began to be resumed; and that, after a short period of ill-feeling and suspicion, circumstances were brought about which enabled both Roman Catholics and other Christians to work without hindrance. In 1872 the interdict against Christianity was formally removed; and the release from imprisonment and return from banishment of hundreds of Christians took place.

Such is the past history of Christianity in Japan. It has, indeed, its elements of glorious and heroic martyrdom, but it has elements, also, on which few of us can look back without a deep sense of shame. Let us trust that by this time the people of Japan have come to understand that the conflict of their forefathers was not with Christianity, but rather with Christians who had forgotten "what spirit they were of."

Turning now to the condition of Christian Missions at the present day, it seems right to commence with those of the Roman Church. Not only has the Roman Church in Japan a history which extends over three hundred years, but it reckons at the present time considerably more than double the number of adherents claimed by any other Christian body. The Roman influence has been particularly successful in the Goto Islands, in the neighbourhood of Nagasaki, where the devoted labours of the missionaries have won over a considerable portion of the population.

To come to the statistics. These give one Archbishop, three Bishops, seventy-eight missionary, and fifteen native priests, with over 300 (native) minor clergy and catechists; 185 churches and chapels, with 244 congregations. Seventy-six sisters of the Order of St. Paul de Chartres are stationed in Japan, and there are further nineteen native novices. Other statistics include seventeen orphanages, with an average of over 100 children; twenty Industrial Schools; eight Nursing establishments; a Hospital for the Aged; and a Hospital for Lepers, with sixty-two inmates, situated at Gotemba, at the foot of Fuji-san. The number of infant baptisms for 1892 is given as, children of Christian parents 1,337, and Heathen parents 1,166; these, with 2,806 adult baptisms, and forty-five "conversions of heretics," bringing the total of baptisms and conversions for the year to 5,354. The work that is being done by the Roman missionaries is commended on all sides; a prominent feature in their methods being a consideration for, and adaptation to, the habits and prejudices of the people, that greatly facilitate their progress, especially among the poor of the country districts. The whole number of Roman Catholics in Japan amounts, as has been said already, to about 45,000.

I pass on to speak of the condition of the Greek, or Orthodox Russian, Church in Japan; whose relations with the Church of England are here, as elsewhere, of a friendly though not, of course, of a very intimate character. Its head-quarters are at Tokio, where an imposing Cathedral, situated on high ground and in a central position, has recently been erected. Unfortunately our information in this case is very incomplete; but assuming the correctness of the numbers before us, one is struck by the paucity of missionary clergy, viz. one bishop and three priests. To these must be added eighteen native clergy, and 128 unordained teachers and workers. There are in all 219 congregations. The number of adult baptisms in 1892 is given as 952; and the total membership at the present time exceeds 20,000. Scanty as these details are, they indicate much activity and progress. The proximity of Russian territory to Japan—Vladivostock being only some 700 miles N. of Nagasaki—is, of course, a circumstance highly favourable to the Orthodox Mission.

Coming now to the various bodies arranged by Mr. Loomis under the title of "Protestant," we will take first the *Nippon Sei Kokwai*, or Church of Japan, which is the name given to the union formed by the Missions of the American Episcopal Church, the Church of England, and the English Church in Canada. It is, however, only fair to say that the total number of adherents of the Nippon Sei Kokwai are greatly less than half the number claimed by the Presbyterian Churches, as also by the Churches of the American Board's Mission. The Missions, then, of the American Church and of the Church of England are to a great extent worked independently of each other, each being under its own Episcopal control; but at the same time, the two Churches enjoy, of course, full intercommunion, and are practically one,— often taking counsel together, and dividing the various districts by mutual arrangement in such a way as to make the best use of their resources. To the American Church belongs the honour of being the first body to commence Christian work in Japan in the present century; the Rev. C. M. Williams, afterwards Bishop for Japan and China, establishing himself at Tokio in 1859, and proceeding at once to translate portions of the Bible and Prayer-Book, hold services for the benefit of English-speaking people, and set on foot schemes for the study of our language. There are now twelve missionary clergy at work, and twenty-one female missionaries; together with seven native clergy and nineteen unordained workers and preachers. Of the

[To face page 138.

SKETCH MAP.

twenty-seven organized churches only one is wholly self-supporting. The number of baptisms in 1892 was, adults 208, children fifty-eight; while the total membership amounts to over 1,400, with a like number of children receiving instruction in Sunday Schools. In 1873, Dr. Henry Laming was appointed missionary physician, and arrived at Osaka, where he has done and is still doing an excellent work. A good deal of secular educational work is also carried on in connexion with the mission.

We next come to the work of the Church Missionary Society, which commenced operations in Japan in 1869. The Society has now twenty-two missionary and seven native clergy engaged; forty-two female missionaries, and sixty unordained preachers. Of its sixteen organized churches one is self-supporting. The number of baptisms in 1892 was, adults 267, children 121; and the total membership at the present time amounts to 2,126, with 600 children in Sunday Schools.

The Society for the Propagation of the Gospel commenced work in 1873; and has its headquarters at Tokio. The work of the two Community Missions, founded by Bishop Bickersteth in 1887, is apparently included in the statistics assigned to the S. P. G. in the table before us. At St. Andrew's University Mission, five clergy—all of whom are University Graduates,—live in community with several native students preparing for Ordination, while at St. Hilda's Mission, a staff of English ladies is engaged in work, which includes schools, a hospital, and a home for mission women. Both these Missions are supported by the 'Guild of St. Paul,'—a society which has branches all over England,—whose occasional papers are full of interesting information. Several other priests of the S. P. G. are engaged at various mission stations; and these, with seven native ministers, make in all some nineteen clergy at work in Japan. The adult baptisms in 1892 numbered 151, and the membership at the present time is given as 784.

The Wyckliffe College Mission was sent out by the Canadian Church in 1888. At present it provides only three clergy, who are engaged at Nagoya, a flourishing commercial city situated about midway between Kyoto and Tokio. Bishop Bickersteth, however, in his recent Pastoral Letter, refers to its work in hopeful and appreciative terms.

The total number of adherents of the Nippon Sei Kokwai will thus be seen to be about 4,300 (with upwards of 2,000 Sunday Scholars); and of these the Church of England can claim barely 3,000. At the same time evidence is by no means lacking that the work is being carried on upon thoroughly sound principles and along right lines; and there are many reasons for believing that, with adequate resources. a future awaits it, under God, far exceeding the calculations that might be suggested by its present numerical strength. Some of the readers of these pages may, possibly, be in greater sympathy with the general position of the S. P. G. than of the C. M. S; but no consideration of this sort should allow us to be inappreciative of the splendid work which the C. M. S. has done in the past, and is still doing in non-Christian countries. Its chief centre in Japan is at Osaka, another huge commercial city, some twenty miles from Kyoto where there is a considerable European settlement. Bishop Bickersteth—as does also the American Bishop, Dr. Williams [1]—resides at Tokio, the capital; where the services at St. Andrew's Church, adjoining the Episcopal residence, are such as may well gladden the heart of an English Churchman, who finds himself 11,000 miles from home. They include, I may mention, a Daily Celebration. A striking feature of the Nippon Sei Kokwai is presented in its Biennial Synods, three, if not four, of which have already been held. The Synods are composed of clergy and laity, every congregation of twenty

---

[1] In the course of the present year (1893), the Rev. J. McKim has been raised to the American Episcopate in Japan; Dr. Williams continuing to reside at Tokio. It is also announced that two new Anglican Bishops are to be consecrated for the Islands of Kyushu and Yezo respectively. One of these is the Rev. H. Evington, Examining Chaplain to Bishop Bickersteth, who has been connected with the C. M. S. Mission to Japan since 1874.

persons being entitled to send its representative; and they indicate a stage of organization rarely, if ever, attained to by so youthful a Church. In a word, what is being aimed at throughout is not to Europeanize, but to Christianize; not to form a "branch of the Church of England," but to establish, on those lines of Catholic and Apostolic Christianity which we believe the Church of England faithfully represents, a *Japanese Church*, which may be committed, as soon as ever circumstances allow, entirely into the hands of the Japanese themselves.

The Bishop's Pastoral Letter to his Clergy (Advent 1892) treats, among other matters, of the Marriage Law of the Church, of Old Testament Criticism,—in the course of his comments upon which, he makes the quotation, "The central object of our Faith is not the Bible, but our Lord"— and of the Bishop of Lincoln's case. It exhibits throughout a tone of earnest Catholicity, of sanctified prudence, and of Apostolic charity. The Bishop's observations on the confirmation by the Privy Council of the Lambeth Judgment will be read with satisfaction by many:—

"The principle of allowed variety in matters of ritual has now been authoritatively recognized. Such recognition is essential to the welfare of a great and living Church in our day. Among other good results which may follow from the decision, I cannot but hope will be the liberation of the energies and interests of a great and historic party, hitherto far too closely confined within the boundaries of our own country, for wider and more extended work, above all in eastern countries. Its own position is now legally secured. Any outstanding questions of ritual could be speedily settled by the application to them of the same principles which are embodied in the recent judgments. This is so plain that probably no such decisions will be challenged. May it not then be hoped that there will shortly be a marked cessation of controversy at home, as for some years past we are told there has been in our sister Church in the United States, and coincidently a far more determined effort on the part of the whole Church than has yet been known, inspired and sustained by the Holy Spirit of Truth, to win the East to the Faith of Christ?"

We come next to the *Church of Christ in Japan*, another amalgamation of religious bodies; comprising, in this case, the Presbyterian Church of the United States, two or three other American sects, and the United Presbyterian Church of Scotland. By far the greater number of denominations engaged in Japan are of American origin; and this is, practically, an American work; the Scotch Presbyterians being represented by only two missionaries with a single station, and only joining the Mission in 1875—fifteen years after two of the

American bodies had commenced their work. The number of male missionaries in connexion with this movement amounts to fifty-two; and to these must be added fifty-three native ministers, 100 female missionaries, and over 100 lay preachers and workers. Of the seventy-four organized churches no less than one-third are wholly self-supporting. Baptisms in 1892 were, adults 789, children 100; and the total present membership amounts to 11,190, with over 2,000 children in Sunday Schools. The fact that the Presbyterians of Japan have recently adopted the Apostles' Creed as their Confession of Faith, in place of the formularies with which their bodies have hitherto been associated, is hardly the occasion for satisfaction that would at first sight appear; the course in question being, I understand, to some extent due to the prevalence of views similar to those held by a large number of the Congregationalists of Japan, to which I shall presently refer. The work of the Presbyterians however, must be accounted among the most successful efforts for the evangelization of the country; while they have had from the beginning the advantage of being supported by men of national reputation and position.

We come now to the *Kumi-ai Churches* in connexion with the American Board's Mission; i.e. the Congregationalists. This work owes its foundation to a Japanese gentleman,—a Mr. Neesima,—who was converted to Christianity, whilst on a visit to America. Its head-quarters are at Kyoto. Starting in 1869—several years after the Presbyterians, their relations with whom are of a cordial character,—the Congregationalists very closely approach them in numerical strength. The Mission is worked by twenty-six missionary and twenty-eight native ministers; with fifty-seven female missionaries and 100 lay agents. Of ninety-two organized churches one half are self-supporting; a large proportion of the converts belonging to the middle and upper classes. 1,096 adults were baptized in 1892 and sixty-six children. Total adherents 10,700, with upwards of 6,000 children in Sunday Schools. In connexion with this Mission is a large college, in which the greater number of the students are Christians, and many of these candidates for the ministry; and mention must also be made of two hospitals under the care of missionary physicians. The above figures, without doubt, bear witness to great energy on the part of the Congregationalist body; and it is with regret that we find ourselves compelled to regard them with somewhat modified satisfaction.

"Speaking generally, it cannot be too clearly felt that systems which do not definitely teach the truths contained in the Apostolic and Nicene Creeds, whatever benefits may accrue to individuals from the moral teaching which they impart, are

not merely negative in tendency and results, but retard the progress of the Kingdom of Christ in Eastern lands." Such are the weighty words of Bishop Bickersteth [1], the occasion which drew them forth being the adoption by the Congregationalists of Japan of the following Declaration of Belief:—
" We believe (i) in the One God, (ii) in Jesus Christ who came on earth to save sinners, (iii) in the Holy Spirit from Whom we receive new life, (iv) in the Bible which shews us the way of salvation, and (v) in Baptism and the Holy Supper, in punishments and rewards given by God according to our merits, in everlasting life if we are righteous, and in the Resurrection of the Dead." Several of the clauses in this statement are open to grave objection; but the fact that the second clause was deliberately adopted in place of the words, "in Jesus Christ, the Only-Begotten Son of God, Who suffered and died to atone for the sins of the world "—an alteration which was heartily welcomed by the Unitarians of Japan—is full of painful significance. The Bishop, while expressing his thankfulness that there are large numbers in the Congregationalist body, who have no share in the prevailing scepticism, points out that in dealing with others, with whom this is not the case, nothing can be gained by any attempt at co-operation. "At such times a severe exclusiveness

[1] *Pastoral Letter to his Clergy*, Advent, 1892.

may be the truest exhibition of a heartfelt sympathy."

To the remaining Missions at work in Japan we can only very briefly refer. The American Methodist Episcopal Church has eighteen missionaries and twenty-nine native ministers; fifty-eight churches; and a total following of nearly 4,000, exclusive of children in Sunday Schools. The Canadian Methodists number over 1,800 adults; and the Baptist Missionary Union (U.S.A.) about 1,300. Two other American sects place their total at 500 each. The German Swiss Protestants number 240; the "Universalists" seventy-eight; and the Society of Friends (U.S.A.) forty-three. The Scandinavian Church, whose mission has only recently commenced its work, has seven clergy engaged; and the Unitarians are represented by two ministers—my only reason for mentioning these last-named bodies together being that no further particulars of either are to hand.

But it is time to be bringing these remarks to a conclusion. We may, then, declare the total number in Japan of those professing Christianity in any form—[I should, by the way, have mentioned that the number of male converts would appear to exceed by about one-third the number of women,]—to be not more than 100,000; while the entire population of the country is estimated at from thirty-eight to forty millions. In other words, not more than one person in every 400 can be said to be, in any sense, a Christian. I emphasize this fact, not because I think it discouraging, but because it seems becoming the fashion for the cause of Christianity in Japan to be spoken of as already won. That Japan has still great changes and developments to undergo in the near future scarcely admits of question. "The nation is working out its spiritual redemption;" and, as Mr. Loomis well says in his letter to *The Christian* before referred to, " As Japanese society advances, there will be all the more a place for Christian influence. *The social problems of the people can only find solution through religion.*" We may well believe and hope that, as time goes on, the true faith of Jesus Christ and of His Church will more and more prevail. So, too, we may rejoice that the foundations have been laid, and that some real and steady progress has been effected; we may hope that more is, even now, being accomplished by the leaven of influence than can at present find place in tables and statistics. And yet, as we look the position boldly in the face, we must see that elements to occasion anxiety are by no means lacking ; and especially must we see how much more remains to be done that has already been achieved. The possibility of some form of Christianity being adopted as the national religion, is a matter as to the desirability of which it is extremely difficult to express an opinion, until the proposition assumes a more definite shape than is likely for some time to be the case.

That both Christianity and Christians are subjected to searching criticism at the hands of the more educated natives we have already seen; while, from time to time, tidings are received of bitter opposition encountered by those engaged in the work of evangelization among the poor of the country districts. Moreover, in that spirit of accommodation to which we have several times referred, as forming so striking a feature of the system, Buddhism appears now to be striving to maintain its position in Japan, by a re-statement of its doctrines in such terms as to place itself in accordance with the modern systems of philosophy, which have found such favour and acceptance with the educated classes. At the same time, there is, without doubt, a widespread persuasion throughout Japan—in many cases most reluctantly arrived at—that the former ascendency of Buddhism has for ever passed away. "A dull apathy as regards religion has settled down upon the educated classes of Japan. The gods of heathenism have crumbled to nothing before modern science and civilization, and the glimmer of light and truth to which they pointed has gone as well[1]." Sometimes, again, Christianity is spoken of by Buddhists in terms which encourage us to hope that there are those

[1] *Occasional Paper*, Guild of St. Paul, Oct. 1893.

who, while they have not as yet taken the decisive step, are still "not far from the kingdom of God." Take, for examples, these words of a Mr. Nakanishi. "It is the glory of mankind that Jesus lived. Much that Christ taught will never decay. Did Christ's teaching come from man, or from above man? Every word, every phrase, of Christ should influence us. In the Four Gospels, the noblest and wisest morality of the world appears. So simple is it, so easily understood and applied. 'Love God and love man,' as central principles, suffice to regenerate society and lead men to heaven. Christ's character and teachings stand for ever."

With a brief reference to one or two further points suggested by Mr. Loomis' table, I will bring this, my last chapter, to a close. One of these is the distinction he draws—and it is a distinction quite worth drawing—between married and unmarried missionaries. Of course, the Roman clergy are all unmarried, as are also the four missionaries of the Orthodox Church; but when we come to the "Protestant Missions," we find the numbers of married and unmarried clergy to be 205 and thirty-seven respectively. Indeed, with the exception of the Church of England, the Scandinavian Alliance, and the American Methodist Episcopal Church, which supply six each, there is no mission with more than two unmarried clergy, and several have not even one. Now it is certain that this is not the way in which great mission work has been done in the past; but is the newer way better than the old? Beyond observing that the presence of female missionaries is in a very special degree needed in Japan, be they the wives of the clergy or not, I will not presume to answer that question myself; but I may, perhaps, be allowed to record the opinion, emphatically expressed to me, of one who has lived in the East for a great many years, and is by no means in sympathy with the compulsory celibacy of the Roman priesthood. "It is," he remarked, "far too hastily assumed that the fact of the married missionary usually bringing another valuable ally to the work sufficiently determines the question. But I am convinced that, speaking generally, it is to the unmarried missionary that wider opportunities of usefulness are extended. Nor is it merely that his movements are entirely free and unhampered—that he is exempt from domestic obligations and anxieties—that he has more time for study—and that he is thrown more in the society of his brother clergy. As a man's children begin to grow up, educational and other considerations in connexion with these, urge upon him the desirability of returning home, with the result that, just as he has begun to master the difficulties of language, and to enter into the thought and habits of the people, his place is taken by a tyro, who, however well-meaning, cannot but have all his experience to gain." No doubt, there is plenty of room for both married and unmarried clergy in the mission field; but the great preponderance of the married in the case before us may well serve to suggest the consideration:— Might not more of that large and possibly increasing number of unmarried clergy in England be drawn to take part in a work of such fascinating interest —"*a work*," if I may once more quote the words of our Bishop in Japan, "*that must be done at once if it is to be done at all.*"

Another point that can scarcely fail to strike us as we examine Mr. Loomis' statistics, is the large number of "dismissals and exclusions" made by those bodies which supply information under this head, and amounting in some cases to several hundreds in a year. That such measures are not resorted to without grave reason may be assumed, and that some exercise of discipline is especially necessary in dealing with a young and nascent church admits of no dispute. There is indeed every reason to hope that by far the greater number of converts are actuated by an intense sincerity, and evidence of this is afforded in the self-sacrifice to which they, in many ways, readily submit for the Faith they have embraced. But, at the same time, it is probable that the numbers in question indicate an even larger proportion of "failures," than is the case with mission work generally; and that they point not only to losses through "back-sliding," but to many instances of insincerity on the part of those professing conversion. It has been remarked that it does not belong to the Japanese temperament to "take things *au grand sérieux*"; and this characteristic extends to matters of religion. The young fellow, for instance, who, for some reason or another, thinks it "worth his while" to conform to Christianity for a time, will have the very smallest scruples about doing so; and that, with a semblance of earnestness that will baffle, at any rate for some time, the careful scrutiny to which candidates are rightly subjected by most, if not all, of the missionary bodies. The missionaries, I fear, are often imposed on; and yet—anything, surely, is better than being over suspicious and severe. After all, what we want to do is to show these different nations to whom we go, that Christ and His Church, and we, His members, do really care for them, alike in things temporal and eternal. Our Faith, to be really preached, needs to be boldly, hopefully practised. And especially in Japan, where the only idea that such a phrase as "eternal life" would commonly suggest is that of a series of painful and endless transmigrations, must Christianity be ready to prove herself man's friend in the things of this life, if she would be looked to with confidence for the things that lie beyond.

PUBLICATIONS

OF THE

SOCIETY FOR PROMOTING CHRISTIAN KNOWLEDGE.

PUBLICATIONS
OF THE
SOCIETY FOR PROMOTING CHRISTIAN KNOWLEDGE.

	s.	d.
Aids to Prayer. By the Rev. DANIEL MOORE. Printed in red and black. Post 8vo. ....*Cloth boards*	1	6
Authenticity of the Gospel of St. Luke (The). Its bearing upon the Evidences of the Truth of Christianity. Five Lectures by the Bishop of Bath and Wells. Small Post 8vo. ....*Cloth boards*	1	6
Being of God, Six Addresses on the. By C. J. ELLICOTT, D.D., Bishop of Gloucester and Bristol. Small Post 8vo. ....*Cloth boards*	1	6
Bible Places; or, The Topography of the Holy Land. By the Rev. Canon TRISTRAM. With Map and numerous Woodcuts. Crown 8vo. ....*Cloth boards*	4	0
Called to be Saints. The Minor Festivals Devotionally Studied. By CHRISTINA G. ROSSETTI, Author of "Seek and Find." Post 8vo. ....*Cloth boards*	5	0
Case for "Establishment" stated (The). By the Rev. T. MOORE, M.A. Post 8vo. *Paper boards*	0	6
Christians under the Crescent in Asia. By the Rev. E. L. CUTTS, B.A., Author of "Turning-Points of Church History," &c. With numerous Illustrations. Crown 8vo. ....*Cloth boards*	5	0
Christus Comprobator; or, The Testimony of Christ to the Old Testament. Seven Addresses by C. J. ELLICOTT, D.D., Bishop of Gloucester and Bristol. Post 8vo. ...*Cloth boards*	2	0

PUBLICATIONS OF THE SOCIETY

	s.	d.
Church History in England. From the Earliest Times to the Period of the Reformation. By the Rev. ARTHUR MARTINEAU, M.A. 12mo. ....*Cloth boards*	3	0
Church History, Sketches of. From the First Century to the Reformation. By the late Rev. Canon ROBERTSON. With Map. 12mo. ....*Cloth boards*	2	0
Daily Readings for a Year. By ELIZABETH SPOONER. Crown 8vo...*Cloth boards*	3	6
Devotional (A) Life of our Lord. By the Rev. E. L. CUTTS, B.A., Author of "Pastoral Counsels," &c. Post 8vo. ....*Cloth boards*	5	0
Face of the Deep (The). A Devotional Commentary on the Apocalypse. By CHRISTINA G. ROSSETTI, Author of "Time Flies." Demy 8vo. ....*Cloth boards*	7	6
Golden Year (The). Thoughts for every Month, Original and Selected. By EMILY C. ORR, Author of "Thoughts for Working Days." Printed in red and black. Post 8vo. *Cloth boards*	1	6
Gospels, the Four. Arranged in the Form of an English Harmony, from the Text of the Authorised Version. By the Rev. J. M. FULLER, M.A. With Analytical Table of Contents and Four Maps. ....*Cloth boards*	1	0
Great Truths and Holy Lives. A Series of Bible Lessons, from Advent to Trinity. By LADY HAMMICK. Post 8vo. ....*Cloth boards*	2	0
History of the English Church. In short Biographical Sketches. By the Rev. JULIUS LLOYD, M.A., Author of "Sketches of Church History in Scotland." Post 8vo. ....*Cloth boards*	1	6

Land of Israel, The. *s. d.*
A Journal of Travel in Palestine, undertaken with special reference to its Physical Character. By the Rev. Canon TRISTRAM. With two Maps and numerous Illustrations. Large Post 8vo. ....*Cloth boards* 10 6

Lectures on the Historical and Dogmatical Position of the Church of England.
By the Rev. W. BAKER, D.D. Post 8vo. *Cloth boards* 1 6

Martyrs and Saints of the first Twelve Centuries.
Studies from the Lives of the Black-letter Saints of the English Calendar. By the Author of "The Schönberg-Cotta Family," &c. Crown 8vo. ....*Cloth boards* 5 0

Paley's Evidences.
A New Edition, with Notes, Appendix, and Preface. By the Rev. E. A. LITTON. Post 8vo. *Cloth boards* 4 0

Paley's Horæ Paulinæ.
A New Edition, with Notes, Appendix, and Preface. By the Rev. J. S. HOWSON, D.D., Dean of Chester. Post 8vo. ....*Cloth boards* 3 0

Peace with God.
A Manual for the Sick. By the Rev. E. BURBIDGE, M.A. Post 8vo. ....*Cloth boards* 1 6

"Perfecting Holiness."
By the Rev. E. L. CUTTS, B.A. Post 8vo. *Cloth boards* 2 6

Plain Words for Christ.
Being a Series of Readings for Working Men. By the late Rev. R. G. DUTTON. Post 8vo. *Cloth boards* 1 0

Readings on the First Lessons for Sundays and Chief Holy Days.

According to the New Table. By the Rev. PETER YOUNG. Crown 8vo. ....*In two volumes* **6 0**

Religion for Every Day.

Lectures for Men. By the Right Rev. A. BARRY, D.D. Fcap. 8vo. ....*Cloth boards* **1 0**

Scenes in the East.

Consisting of Twelve Coloured Photographic Views of Places mentioned in the Bible, beautifully executed, with Descriptive Letterpress. By the Rev. Canon TRISTRAM. ....*Cloth, bevelled boards, gilt edges* **6 0**

Seek and Find.

A Double Series of Short Studies of the Benedicite. By CHRISTINA G. ROSSETTI. Post 8vo. *Cloth boards* **2 6**

Servants of Scripture, The.

By the late Rev. JOHN W. BURGON, B.D. Post 8vo. *Cloth boards* **1 6**

Sinai and Jerusalem: or Scenes from Bible Lands.

Coloured Photographic Views of Places mentioned in the Bible, including a Panoramic View of Jerusalem, with Descriptive Letterpress. By the Rev. F. W. HOLLAND. Demy 4to. *Cloth, bevelled bds., gilt edges* **6 0**

Some Chief Truths of Religion.

By the Rev. EDWARD L. CUTTS, B.A., Author of "St. Cedd's Cross," &c. Crown 8vo. ......*Cloth boards* **2 6**

Spiritual Counsels; or Helps and Hindrances to Holy Living.

By the late Rev. R. G. DUTTON, M.A. Post 8vo. *Cloth boards* **1 0**

FOR PROMOTING CHRISTIAN KNOWLEDGE. 5

| | s. | d. |

Thoughts for Men and Women.
THE LORD'S PRAYER. By EMILY C. ORR. Post 8vo.
Limp cloth 1 0

Thoughts for Working Days.
Original and Selected. By EMILY C. ORR. Post 8vo.
Limp cloth 1 0

Three Martyrs of the Nineteenth Century.
Studies from the Lives of Livingstone, Gordon, and Patteson. By the Author of "Chronicles of the Schönberg-Cotta Family." Crown 8vo. *Cloth boards* 3 6

Time Flies; a Reading Diary.
By CHRISTINA G. ROSSETTI. Post 8vo. *Cloth boards* 2 6

True Vine (The).
By the Author of "The Schönberg-Cotta Family," &c. Printed in red and black. Post 8vo......*Cloth boards* 1 6

Turning-Points of English Church History.
By the Rev. EDWARD L. CUTTS, B.A., Vicar of Holy Trinity, Haverstock Hill. Crown 8vo. *Cloth boards* 3 6

Turning-Points of General Church History.
By the Rev. E. L. CUTTS, B.A., Author of "Pastoral Counsels," &c. Crown 8vo. ....*Cloth boards* 5 0

NON-CHRISTIAN RELIGIOUS SYSTEMS.

A Series of Manuals which furnish in a brief and popular form an accurate account of the great Non-Christian Religious Systems of the World.

Fcap. 8vo., cloth boards, 2s. 6d. each.

BUDDHISM—BEING A SKETCH OF THE LIFE AND TEACHINGS OF GUATAMA, THE BUDDHA.
By T. W. RHYS DAVIDS. With Map.

BUDDHISM IN CHINA. By the Rev. S. BEAL. With Map.

CHRISTIANITY AND BUDDHISM. A COMPARISON AND A CONTRAST.
By the Rev. T. STERLING BERRY, D.D.

CONFUCIANISM AND TAOUISM.
By Professor ROBERT K. DOUGLAS, of the British Museum. With Map.

HINDUISM. By Professor MONIER WILLIAMS. With Map.

ISLAM AND ITS FOUNDER. By J. W. H. STOBART. With Map.

ISLAM AS A MISSIONARY RELIGION. By C. R. HAINES. (2s.)

THE CORAN—ITS COMPOSITION AND TEACHING, AND THE TESTIMONY IT BEARS TO THE HOLY SCRIPTURES.
By Sir WILLIAM MUIR, K.C.S.I.

THE HEATHEN WORLD AND ST. PAUL.

This Series is intended to throw light upon the Writings and Labours of the Apostle of the Gentiles.

Fcap. 8vo., cloth boards, 2s. each.

ST. PAUL IN GREECE. By the Rev. G. S. DAVIES. With Map.

ST. PAUL IN DAMASCUS AND ARABIA.
By the Rev. GEORGE RAWLINSON, M.A., Canon of Canterbury. With Map.

ST. PAUL AT ROME.
By the Very Rev. CHARLES MERIVALE, D.D., D.C.L., Dean of Ely. With Map.

ST. PAUL IN ASIA MINOR AND AT THE SYRIAN ANTIOCH.
By the late Rev. E. H. PLUMPTRE, D.D. With Map.

CONVERSION OF THE WEST.

A Series of Volumes showing how the Conversion of the Chief Races of the West was brought about, and their condition before this occurred.

Fcap. 8vo., cloth boards, 2s. each.

THE CELTS.
By the Rev. G. F. MACLEAR, D.D. With Two Maps.

THE ENGLISH.
By the above Author. With Two Maps.

THE NORTHMEN.
By the above Author. With Map.

THE SLAVS.
By the above Author. With Map.

THE CONTINENTAL TEUTONS.
By the Very Rev. Dean MERIVALE. With Map.

ANCIENT HISTORY FROM THE MONUMENTS.

This Series of Books is chiefly intended to illustrate the Sacred Scriptures by the results of recent Monumental Researches in the East.

Fcap. 8vo., cloth boards, 2s. each.

ASSYRIA, FROM THE EARLIEST TIMES TO THE FALL OF NINEVEH.
By the late GEORGE SMITH, Esq., of the British Museum.

SINAI: FROM THE FOURTH EGYPTIAN DYNASTY TO THE PRESENT DAY.
By the late HENRY S. PALMER, Major R.E., F.R.A.S. With Map. A new and revised edition by the Rev. Professor SAYCE.

BABYLONIA (THE HISTORY OF).
By the late GEORGE SMITH, Esq. Edited by the Rev. A H. SAYCE.

EGYPT, FROM THE EARLIEST TIMES TO B.C. 300.
By the late S. BIRCH, LL.D.

PERSIA, FROM THE EARLIEST PERIOD TO THE ARAB CONQUEST.
By the late W. S. W. VAUX, M.A.

THE FATHERS FOR ENGLISH READERS.

A Series of Monographs on the Chief Fathers of the Church, the Fathers selected being centres of influence at important periods of Church History and in important spheres of action.

Fcap. 8vo., cloth boards, 2s. each.

LEO THE GREAT.
By the Rev. CHARLES GORE, M.A.

GREGORY THE GREAT.
By the Rev. J. BARMBY, B.D.

SAINT AMBROSE: his Life, Times, and Teaching.
By the Rev. ROBINSON THORNTON, D.D.

SAINT ATHANASIUS: his Life and Times.
By the Rev. R. WHELER BUSH. (2s. 6d.)

SAINT AUGUSTINE.
By the Rev. E. L. CUTTS, B.A.

SAINT BASIL THE GREAT.
By the Rev. RICHARD T. SMITH, B.D.

SAINT BERNARD: Abbot of Clairvaux, A.D. 1091-1153.
By the Rev. S. J. EALES, M.A., D.C.L. (2s. 6d.)

SAINT HILARY OF POITIERS, AND SAINT MARTIN OF TOURS.
By the Rev. J. GIBSON CAZENOVE, D.D.

SAINT JEROME.
By the Rev. EDWARD L. CUTTS, B.A.

SAINT JOHN OF DAMASCUS.
By the Rev. J. H. LUPTON, M.A.

SAINT PATRICK: his Life and Teaching.
By the Rev. E. J. NEWELL, M.A. (2s. 6d.)

SYNESIUS OF CYRENE, Philosopher and Bishop.
By ALICE GARDNER.

THE APOSTOLIC FATHERS.
By the Rev. Canon HOLLAND.

THE DEFENDERS OF THE FAITH; or, The Christian Apologists of the Second and Third Centuries.
By the Rev. F. WATSON, M.A.

THE VENERABLE BEDE.
By the Rev. G. F. BROWNE.

LONDON:—NORTHUMBERLAND AVENUE, W.C.;
43, QUEEN VICTORIA STREET, E.C.;
BRIGHTON: 135, NORTH STREET.

www.ingramcontent.com/pod-product-compliance
Lightning Source LLC
Chambersburg PA
CBHW020056170426
43199CB00009B/303